17.

.Cl

THE COCKPIT OF EUROPE

THE COCKPIT OF EUROPE

A Guide to the Battlefields of Belgium and France

Lt-Colonel Howard Green, MC, FSA

DAVID & CHARLES · NEWTON ABBOT · LONDON · VANCOUVER

HIPPOCRENE BOOKS INC · NEW YORK

HIPPOCRENE
BOOKS, INC.

For
Betty Ryder
with our love

The author gratefully acknowledges the services of his two secretary-typists, Mrs Woodmore of Pagham and Mrs Bone of Felpham. Both possess the four essentials for their work: efficiency, speed, cooperation with a smile, and much appreciated by any author, an interest in the subject.

This edition first published in 1976 in Great Britain by David & Charles (Holdings) Limited, Newton Abbot, Devon and in the United States of America in 1976 by Hippocrene Books Inc., 171 Madison Avenue, New York, N.Y. 10016

Published in Canada by Douglas, David & Charles Limited, 1875 Welch Street, North Vancouver BC

ISBN 0 7153 7006 5 Great Britain
ISBN 0-88254-367-9 United States

Library of Congress Catalog Card Number: 75-29813

Set in Linotype Baskerville
and Printed in Great Britain
by Latimer Trend & Company Ltd Plymouth

Contents

Introduction

There are several colloquial and unofficial phrases in the English language that describe certain areas of the world. The Spanish Main, the Roaring Forties, the South Seas and the Dark Continent are all apt and expressive, but none is more descriptive than the Cockpit of Europe, a phrase coined by James Howell, author and traveller, in 1640.

Many motorists driving from the Channel ports to the sun pass through the Cockpit. They hurry across north-east France or Belgium because they believe the district to be industrialised, flat, dreary and uninviting, and are anxious to leave it behind them. But they are driving through history. Within the quadrilateral formed by Calais, Liège, Nancy and Abbeville lie over thirty battlefields, and no area in the world has seen so many famous engagements or so much history. No wonder it is called the Cockpit of Europe.

The large majority of the battlefields are not built over and are easy of access. At nearly all one or more of the physical features that influenced the action are still visible today.

The amateur historian will enjoy standing on the very spot at Crécy where Edward III said 'Let the boy win his spurs', or where Wellington called out at Waterloo 'Stand up, Guards'. The precise spot at Sedan where Napoleon III and Bismarck met, the tower of the ruined château near Malplaquet whence Marlborough (and Sir Winston Churchill) viewed the battlefield, the farm building at Ramillies with the scars of Marlborough's cannon-balls still showing, the Tranchée des Baionnettes at Verdun, are all still there. To the real enthusiast these sites, previously so remote in time and distance, seem to have been rediscovered and to offer a silent welcome to the visitor.

I have visited every battlefield mentioned in this book, some more than once. Each one never fails to come alive, and to tell me the story again. It is my hope that its readers will obtain as much pleasure, interest, and indeed exercise in 'walking' these battlefields as I have done.

Craigwell Manor
Aldwick
West Sussex

Howard Green

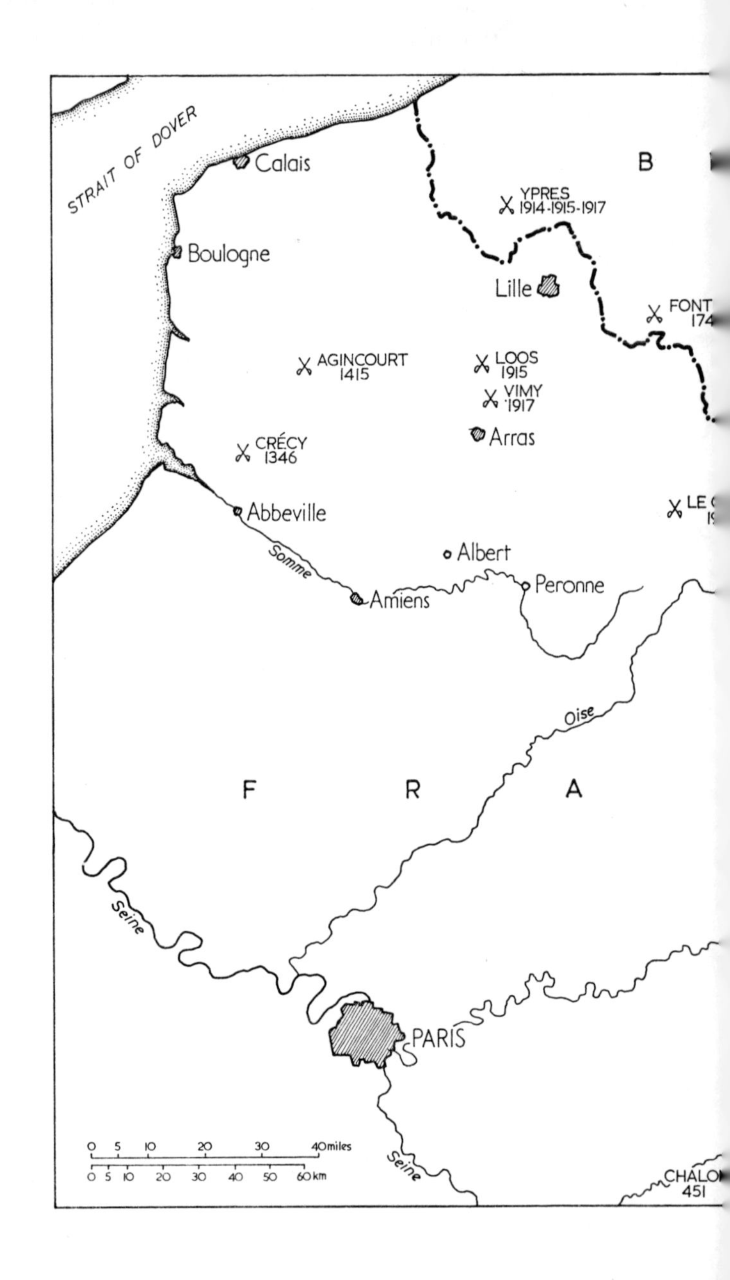
STRAIT OF DOVER
Calais
Boulogne
B
YPRES
1914-1915-1917
Lille
AGINCOURT
1415
LOOS
1915
VIMY
1917
Arras
CRÉCY
1346
Abbeville
Somme
Albert
Amiens
Peronne
Oise
F
R
A
Seine
PARIS
Seine
0 5 10 20 30 40 miles
0 5 10 20 30 40 50 60 km
451

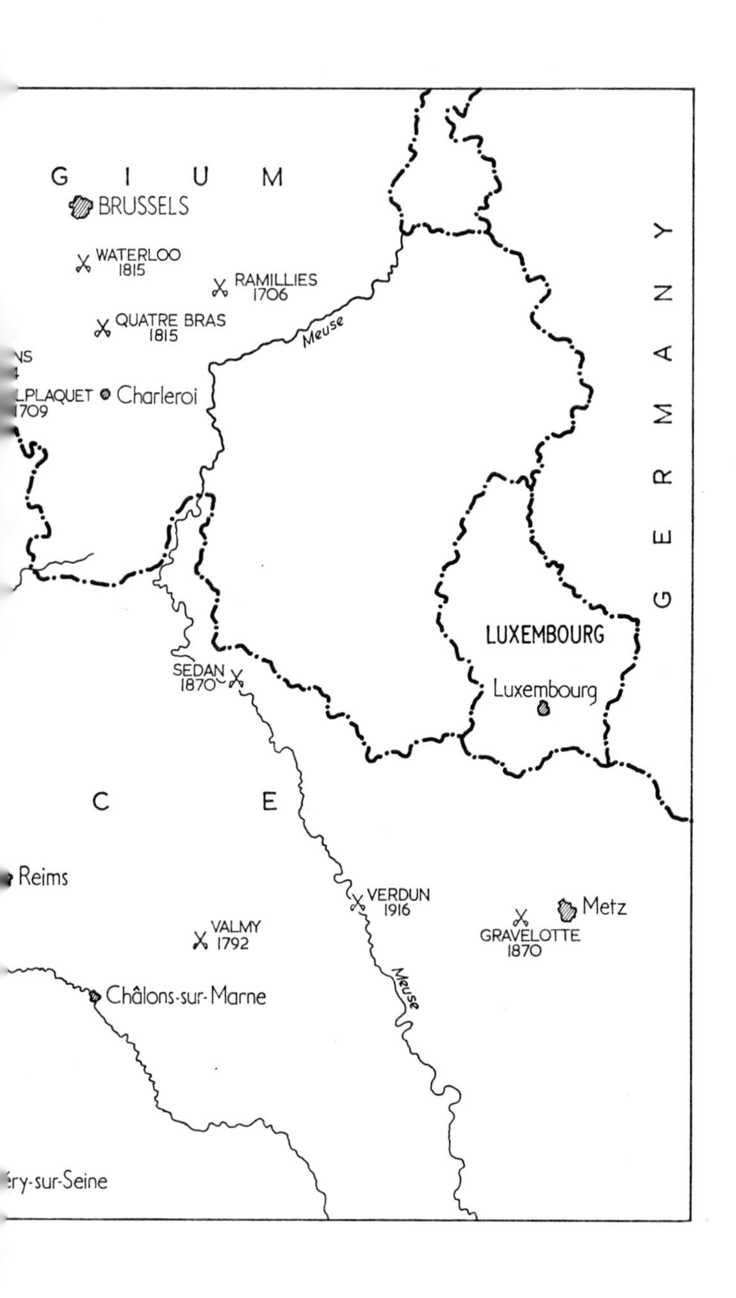
G I U M
BRUSSELS
WATERLOO 1815
RAMILLIES 1706
QUATRE BRAS 1815
Meuse
Charleroi
GERMANY
LUXEMBOURG
Luxembourg
SEDAN 1870
C E
Reims
VERDUN 1916
Metz
GRAVELOTTE 1870
VALMY 1792
Meuse
Châlons-sur-Marne

1 Châlons: AD 451

SITE *About 35 miles south-west of Châlons, and roughly 3 miles south-west of Méry-sur-Seine, Aube, France; it lies 1 mile west of the crossroads, La Belle Etoile, and is crossed by Route Nationale 19, Nogent to Troyes.*
CONTESTANTS *The last Roman army, and the Visigoths under Theodoric, all under the Roman general Aetius. The Huns under Attila, the Scourge of God.*
NUMBERS ENGAGED AND CASUALTIES *Unknown. Probably about 15,000 on each side, the Hun losing some 6,000 men and Aetius perhaps 3,000. All wounded Huns and those captured can safely be assumed to have been murdered by the victors after the battle. A large proportion of the men on each side, perhaps 60 per cent were mounted.*

PRESENT ACCOMMODATION *The Hôtel Croix d'Or at Provins (25 miles westward), and the Grand, or Royal, hotels at Troyes (18 miles south-east) are adequate. Superb motor roads in this district.*

The long, successful and prosperous rule of the Roman Empire had led to a decline in the virility of its people (as has happened often in history and will happen again), creating a love of luxury and an unwillingness to fight and strive to protect the very conditions they had achieved and were enjoying. Roman decadence was noted by the Barbarian peoples in eastern Europe and western Asia, and their pressure on the frontiers of the empire caused Roman withdrawals, the people preferring to surrender territory rather than fight to keep it.

Most of the great antagonists of the empire came from north of the Alps. From present-day Germany, Austria, Poland and western

Russia came the Vandals. From out of the mists of western Asia came the Goths and the Huns. Through the years many of the Vandals forced their way through the Alps, and although often their advance is referred to as the 'Barbarian invasions', it is more accurate to call it the migration of a people of different race, culture and character to that of the Romans. The Goths and Huns came westward across the Balkan Peninsula, sailing up the Danube, while the Vandals passed into Gaul where, in the middle of the fifth century and some years after Britain had been evacuated by the Romans, they roamed at will.

The morale of the Roman army, already fully stretched, had by now fallen considerably. Rome had been captured by Alaric, the Visigoth, but then, luckily for Christendom, the Goths had fallen out among themselves. The campaigns between their various armies did much to weaken them, and in 415 the sudden death of the powerful and warlike Alaric turned the Visigoths into almost a civilised race, far less dangerous than before and much attached to their old Roman adversaries. Indeed, in France, where a large number had settled, many young Visigoths joined the still existing Roman legions, while the original Visigoth army openly allied itself to the official Roman occupation force.

In AD 446 a great Hun invasion swept over northern Europe. The Huns were by far the most cruel and ruthless of all the barbarians. They were almost entirely nomadic. They were contemptuous of civilisation, the arts, and Roman love of order and good government, and could only be kept in control by the hand of a powerful ruthless dictator. They had one in Attila, the Scourge of God.

Attila, was not, as is popularly imagined, just a savage. He was sober in his private life, fair when sitting in judgement, grave and deliberate in council, and rapid and efficient in the execution of his plans. He ruled his many thousands of Huns by sheer strength of personality, and in any age would have been an outstanding figure.

After much martial success in the Balkans, at Byzantium and in eastern Europe, he turned his vast forces towards the conquest of western Europe. The great advance was made in two wings. The northern one reached Arras, while the other moved on to Orléans, which Attila besieged but failed to capture.

In AD 451 the last of the great Roman generals, Aetius, with his mixed force of Romans and Visigoths, was watching Attila at Orléans. His army was imbued both with hatred and dread of the Hun invader, and Attila, seeing or hearing of the high and growing numbers and morale of his enemy, gave up the siege for Orléans and withdrew eastward to the great plain of Châlons, where he took up a defensive position.

The exact whereabouts of this position and the consequent battle has always been a matter of conjecture. There is considerable conflicting evidence for the three possible sites. The first is close to the village of Méry-sur-Seine (lying west of the Seine) and between the villages of Vallant St Georges and Chartres along the line of the modern N19, Troyes to Nogent. What is known of the tactics of the battle fits the physical features of this site, and it is noteworthy that one historian refers to Attila leaving a rearguard west of the river to protect his final withdrawal eastward to Châlons.

The next alternative site is near the village of Pouan, some 9 miles north-west of Méry-sur-Seine. About 120 years ago a French archaeologist uncovered the site of a very ancient grave on the banks of a little brook here flowing into the River Aube. It contained the weapons, armour and jewels of the Visigothic period and clearly had been the burial place of a chieftain. Perhaps it was the grave of King Theodoric, who was killed in the battle. But why did his son and followers go to all the trouble of moving the body 35 miles to a remote spot for burial, and slightly nearer the retreating Huns? The probable site of the encounter at Méry-sur-Seine would do equally well. The burial party, at the conclusion of the battle and with their enemy defeated but by no means routed, would have many pressing dangers on their hands, and a brief though reverent and befitting ceremony would be all they had time for. In any case there is no evidence from the contents of the grave that it was, in fact, Theodoric who was buried there. All that is known is that it was an important Visigoth chieftain.

The third possible site is 8 miles north-east from Châlons and some 45 miles from Méry-sur-Seine. On the Michelin motoring map, between the villages of La Cheppe and Cuperly, appear the words 'Camp d'Attila' with a conventional sign indicating entrenchments 1 mile long.

Sir Edward Creasy in his classic *Fifteen Decisive Battles of the World* says that along this line there are ranges of grassy mounds and trenches which he believes indicate the fortified position of Attila's camp. But this attribution of these earthworks does not bear examination. The walls or ramparts are far older than AD 451. The road signs read 'Prehistoric Circle' and it is evident that the remains date from about 100 BC. They are about 10 feet high and are continuous except for two small breaks where the cart-track, barely passable for a car, enters and leaves the circle. They are largely covered on the top and the outer face by trees and bushes, but their trace is easily determined from any one viewpoint on their top, helped by the entire absence of trees within the walls.

The enclosed circle is about 600 yards in diameter and mostly covered in crops, though one little segment has a football ground marked out, with goalposts, and it is clearly the home ground of La Cheppe. Sir Edward Creasy is sadly inaccurate in describing the great earthwork as 'ranges of grassy mounds and trenches'. They are far more than that. There are no trenches and it is evident that he had not visited the site before writing his account.

An enormous moat outside the ramparts makes them virtually unassailable. The designer of the camp used the little brook, Noblette, flowing close alongside the western and southern facing portions to enhance their impregnability. The walls themselves appear to be entirely of chalk, with no signs of any other building materials such as flints or primitive bricks. A pleasant footpath,

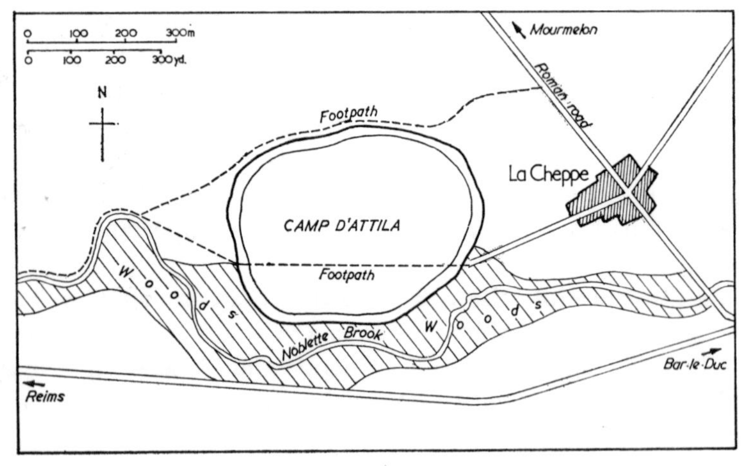

permitting pedestrians to move in single file, follows the top, but care is needed.

The time necessary to build this vast earthwork is difficult to estimate. Certainly hundreds of men must have worked for many weeks, and Attila's stay in this area of but a few days make it quite impossible that his army could have built it. It is highly likely that he withdrew there for shelter after his defeat by Aetius at Méry-sur-Seine, having noted its excellent tactical position as he had previously advanced westward to Orléans.

It seems, therefore, that the first possibility, the position at Méry-sur-Seine, was the probable site of the battle.

Attila's line ran from a quarter of a mile immediately south of Chartres south-east for about a mile, his left being half a mile short of a little hillock of Les Turées and his right resting on the N19 road. He commanded the centre and right, with the Ostrogoths on his left.

Half a mile away to the south-east Aetius formed up his army. On the left he posted the Romans, in the centre some Alans whose courage and loyalty were suspect, and on the right the Visigoths under their king, Theodoric. The line crossed the N19 at an angle, between the crossroads at La Belle Etoile and Chartres. Theodoric sent some cavalry under his son, Thorismond, to hold the little hillock of Les Turées, 50 feet high, out on the right flank and overlooking Attila's line.

After a brief exchange of missiles, mostly stones thrown from slings, Attila himself led his cavalry en masse against the wavering Alans, who broke and fled. Wheeling left, the Huns attacked the Visigoths, trying to take them in rear, but young Thorismond, seeing his father unhorsed in the mêlée, charged them. In this wild charge King Theodoric was knocked down and trampled to death.

Thorismond's charge drove Attila and most of his army back to their original encampment. Aetius wisely did not move his Romans forward, fearing the Hun retreat might be a ruse to tempt him to leave his lines, and he held his post throughout the night, restraining with difficulty his Visigoths from advancing into possible disaster. Attila, now in his own camp, barricaded himself with his wagons, and awaited a dawn attack. But none came and a two-day stalemate ensued, each side suspecting the other of some deep

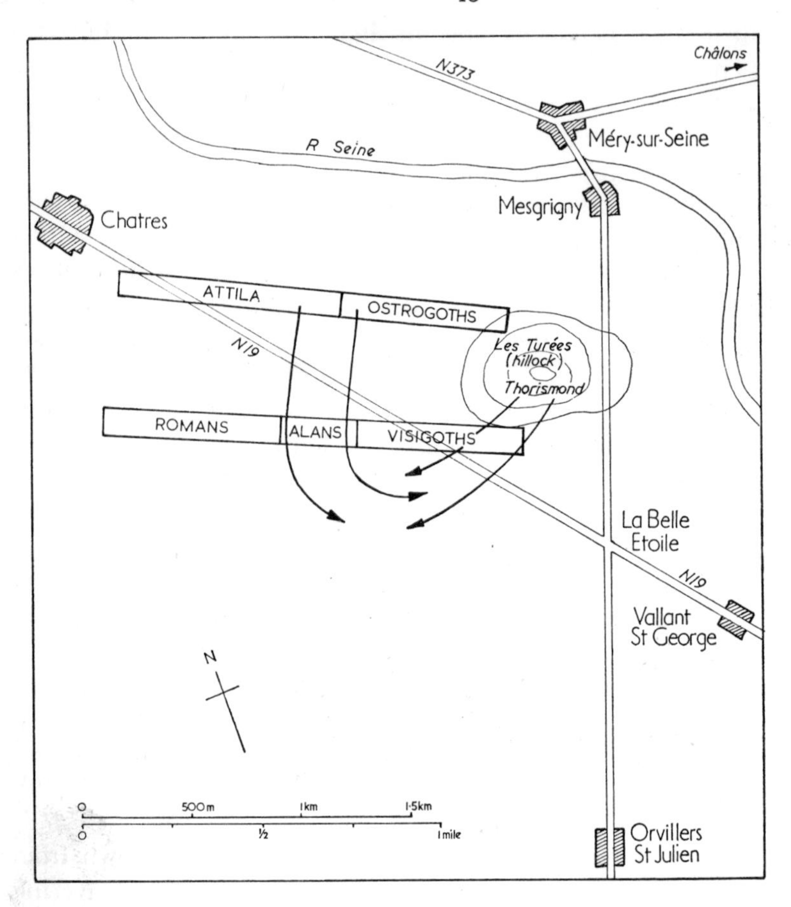

tactical surprise. Eventually Aetius withdrew slightly and Attila marched away to safety, probably pausing to rest and reorganise in the Camp d'Attila on his way eastward to the Rhine and thence the Danube.

Aetius had acted skilfully by not attacking the Huns. Had he done so with success, the whole Hunnish army might well have been dispersed and the threat to Gaul been removed; then the Visigoths would not have needed to cooperate with the last Roman army against a common enemy. Aetius knew that the disappearance of the Hun menace might easily persuade his Visigoths to join forces with other Goths and thereby constitute a new and serious threat to his Roman army and the dying empire.

In AD 452 Attila moved down into northern Italy, which he

ravaged, and then a year later he died of a heart attack. His savage ill-disciplined army was held together only by his masterful personality. When this was suddenly removed, it disintegrated and the Huns were never again a serious threat to Rome, the West, or western Christianised civilisation.

The Battle of Châlons was one of the decisive battles of history. It possessed both the qualifications necessary for it to be included in that small category. Firstly, it was decisive because it saw the end of utter military domination by one power, Rome, over its neighbours, which had lasted for several centuries. Although Châlons was a victory for Roman arms, it was not only the last victory but also Rome's last great battle. Châlons was indeed the swansong of a nation that had brought law, order, good government, prosperity, justice and great civilisation to the world. Probably we today owe more to the Pax Romana than to any other single happening. Châlons saw the end of this great era.

The victory of Châlons may be called decisive, secondly, because victory for the Huns would have demonstrably altered the course of history. Roman power in western Europe, already waning, would have been ruthlessly extinguished, and the timidly expanding Christianity obliterated. The heathen creed of the Huns would have been enforced on the French, Spanish and German peoples, and there can be little doubt that after a while the British Isles would have been invaded and the Asiatic paganism of the Huns established here. But the victory of the Romans and Visigoths in repelling and defeating the Huns saved western Europe from becoming a desert empty of ideas, religion, civilisation and advancement. The Huns had created such conditions in Asia and, indeed, everywhere they had paused – deserts that were to take centuries to flower again.

The visitor should drive slowly from La Belle Etoile, an important crossroads, where the N19 crosses the D7, towards Chartres. He can then be certain that he is passing between the two opposing lines at the start of the battle. The little hillock where Thorismond and his cavalry were first posted affords a good view of the whole battlefield. It lies a quarter of a mile to the west of the road running from La Belle Etoile to Mesgrigny.

2 Crécy: 1346

SITE *Twelve miles north of Abbeville, 3 miles west from the N28.*
CONTESTANTS *The English army, under Edward III, of about 25,000 men with 5,000 horses (mostly pack-horses, not battle-worthy). The French army under King Philip VI of 55,000, of whom 3,000 were mounted knights. Philip had a large contingent of professional Genoese crossbowmen. Their new weapon was considered by the Pope to be an outrage in civilised warfare (comparable to the use of poison gas by the Germans in 1915?).*
CASUALTIES *The French lost 20,000 men, largely to the English archers. The English lost less than 1,000.*

PRESENT ACCOMMODATION *Hôtel France in Abbeville is excellent. Crécy is a charming little town, with country shops but no hotel. Roads excellent.*

The Battle of Crécy was the first great victory in British history. It ranks with Blenheim and Waterloo as one of the three supreme achievements of the British army.

The real object of Edward III's invasion of the Continent in 1346 was not so much to secure the throne of France and establish a great Anglo-French monarchy under the Plantagenets, as to undertake a bold venture and revenge himself on the French king who had repudiated his claim to the throne.

Edward's army of 25,000 men with 5,000 horses embarked at Southampton, and on the following day, 12 July, started to disembark near Cherbourg. These two operations must have been tremendous undertakings. The comparatively small ships of those days did not carry more than a few hundred men each, or perhaps a hundred horses, and so probably not less than sixty troopships and fifty horse-boats must have converged on the landing beach. To land the horses on an open beach, as they did, at St Vaast, must have taken many hours. As each ship grounded, whether at high tide or low, it must have listed considerably, throwing the horses off balance – and probably off their legs. It must have been a lengthy process leading them down the very roughly improvised gangways, or, if each horse was 'slung' over the side into shallow water, that must have taken just as long. The men in the ranks with their longbows and stores of arrows, the cumbersome spears, and armour, probably tentage and the baggage inseparable from such a large force must all have needed not only time and organisation to disembark but also much beach space.

The army rested for a week where it had landed. Barfleur was sacked, Cherbourg attacked, and the countryside ravaged, and on 18 July the march to the south-east started. In the next twenty-seven days the army marched 215 miles – an average of 8 miles a day – before arriving at the crossing of the Seine at Poissy, 12 miles below Paris. Here the bridge was found to be practicable, though two days were spent in repairing it, and the army crossed on 15 August.

At Poissy, however, Edward heard that the French army of 55,000 was in and near Paris. Clearly withdrawal was inevitable and he turned north for the English Channel. Philip learnt the facts two days later and started in pursuit. What followed was a fine feat of marching.

In making for the coast the crossing of the Somme was unavoidable, and in five days Edward covered 85 miles to Abbeville, where he intended to cross the river. However, the bridges there and for several miles further downstream were held in strength by detached French local forces and by 23 August Edward with his whole army concentrated under his hand, but very tired, was faced with a desperate situation. An enemy twice his strength was close behind him and in front was an unfordable river, every bridge over which was denied to him.

At Boismont, near St Valery, on the night of 23 August, a French peasant was brought to the King, saying that he knew of a ford only 2 miles away which at low tide was fully usable. Edward, now faced by the possibility of surrender to a numerically superior enemy, took the chance, his only chance.

Having marched at dawn on the 24th, the army found the ford of Blanchetaque covered in water and still too deep to permit a crossing. The tide was ebbing, however, and by 9 am the way across could be seen. The crossing took several hours, for 30,000 men, mostly on foot, with wagons, tents, reserve of armour and weapons, and by no means least the plunder wagons, all had to be marshalled into a narrow column. This was another great feat of organisation, and time was against it. The tide would rise again and the French come up from the rear. This they did as the main body of the transport, with an insufficient rearguard, was crossing. It was cut off and captured, but the whole of the fighting troops were over, and the tide now prevented any pursuit for at least five hours.

The English moved away from the river and reached the town of Crécy early in the morning of the 26th. Here the army took up a good defensive position, Edward having decided to turn and fight now that his way to the cost and possible re-embarkation lay clear. The ridge the army occupied faces east and west, and at its southern end slopes sharply down into the town. The eastern slope levels out after 300 yards, into the Val aux Clercs, and then rises again to a second broad ridge. The Val aux Clercs peters out as it progresses northward between the two ridges, and the head of the valley is really the head of a broad 'U', its opening being to the south. Beyond the base of the 'U' is the village of Wadicourt. On the southern end of the ridge nearest to the town stood a windmill.

The English took up a series of lines on the eastern slope of the western ridge, facing eastward across the Val aux Clercs, and in front were the archers, the forefathers of the riflemen of Mons and Le Cateau. The line bent back to its right rear round the shoulder overlooking Crécy town, and Edward established his headquarters at the mill, whence he could see the whole of the ridges. About half way up the valley a re-entrant protruded into the English line, and the line of archers conformed to it. The Black Prince, Edward III's son, aged fifteen, commanded the right flank where it bent round the end of the ridge, facing Crécy town. The mill stood behind him.

Halted by the rising tide at Blanchetaque, the French army piled up along the banks of the Somme. Some of them, finding the various bridges previously denied to the English now open, streamed across the river in a disorganised fashion between the ford at Blanchetaque on the north-west and Abbeville on the south-east, on a frontage of 12 miles.

On the 24th and 25th the French seem to have been leaderless. The majority crossed the river by the ford when the tide receded again. These contingents and those who had crossed by the three bridges above the ford all moved forward blindly, generally veering north-east, and reached the village of Fontaine on the morning of 26 August. From here they could see the British line along the far Crécy ridge, 3 miles away to their left front. Wheeling half left, they advanced for 2 miles, and there halted to form in some sort of order. The English soldiers had had their midday meal and been reviewed by Edward, and were now lying down in their ranks, mostly asleep.

About 5 o'clock the crossbowmen advanced over the low eastern ridge and down into the Val aux Clercs, followed by a large body of French mounted knights. At the foot of the slight slope up to the English lines they halted and opened fire with their crossbows. Instantly the English archers, now standing up, took their one pace forward and poured in that terrible fire of arrows, sustained, accurate, and rapid, which had never been seen before in continental warfare. It was to become a legend in Europe.

The Genoese bowmen fell into disorder, being hopelessly outmatched. A great number turned and fled, throwing the lines of French mounted knights behind them into confusion. Many of these mounted men then rode down the despised Genoese deliberately and, riding on charged the English right, under the Black Prince. Some escaped the fire of the archers and for a while there were a series of mêlées among the English lines. The Prince himself was unhorsed and for a while pressure was severe. In the heat of the confused fighting the Black Prince understandably sent to his father at the mill for help. This Edward refused, adding, 'Let the boy win his spurs'. But the effect of the arrow fire on the majority of the charging cavalry was telling gradually and this first charge melted away.

The second phase of the battle comprised cavalry charges only,

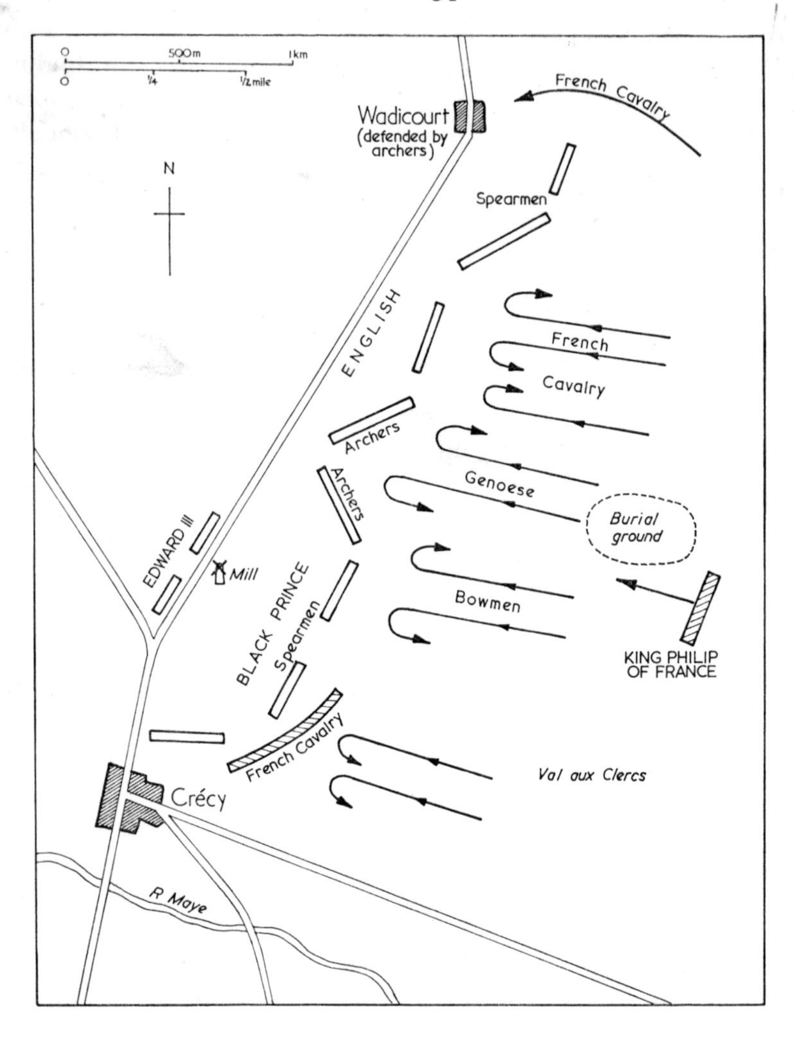

line after line of mounted French knights advancing in successive waves, all to be beaten back by the superb archery of the English. Twelve separate attempts were counted, all unsuccessful.

In the third stage of the battle the French attempted to outflank the English left at Wadicourt. Here the village, with its gardens and orchards, formed an impenetrable though limited obstacle. The archers holding it had little difficulty in repelling the mounted attack, which failed to penetrate anywhere. However, had this well-intentioned flank attack gone further out to its right, beyond the range of the bowmen and then come in boldly on the English left rear, the result must have been important. It is doubtful whether a successful flank attack could have turned the scales at so late a stage, but it must certainly have caused the English much embarrassment.

The last phase of the attack was similar to that of the Old Guard at Waterloo. Led by the King of France in person, a huge force of dismounted men-at-arms advanced westward in the centre, determined to break the line by sheer weight of numbers. The setting sun full in their eyes made the English almost invisible to them, and their attack, too, was held. The right of this last advance made greater progress than any other. It even reached the re-entrant in the English line, and there it met, as intended, not only frontal fire, but fire from both flanks. Not a man in the re-entrant survived.

As darkness fell, King Philip withdrew, and the whole French army fled from the field. For the English the fight was wholly defensive – not a man moved forward except to take the place of a man in front who had fallen – and casualties were under 1,000. Crécy was considered by Sir Winston Churchill to be England's greatest victory over the French, greater even than that of Waterloo.

Throughout the night the enemy wandered aimlessly southward away from the battlefield. The mounted knights rode away in disgust and bitter disappointment. Next morning there was not an unwounded French soldier, officer or man, within 2 miles, except prisoners of war, whose chances of survival in those days were small. During the night the English line broke and moved down into the valley by the light of lanterns to plunder and dispatch the wounded, to loot, and look for the banners and ensigns of the more noble among the dead.

Early next morning the line stood to arms. Through the mist appeared small bodies of Philip's men, recently arrived. A few mounted knights rode out and quickly dispersed them, and all the morning English soldiers killed what wounded they could find.

The extent of the French losses will never be known. A list of 1,500 dead knights alone was made, and the total that fell, largely to the bowmen, was probably 20,000.

On the Monday morning, 28 August, the army resumed its

northward march, now quite free from any danger of pursuit. It reached Calais, which it besieged throughout the winter. In August 1347 the town surrendered.

Today, with the exception of the mill, the whole area of the battlefield is exactly as it was 600 odd years ago. Indeed the mill itself was standing about 80 years ago. It survived long enough to see the birth of photography and to be one of its early subjects. By then, however, it was derelict, and allowed to collapse. There is still a large heap of rubble left, now entirely covered in turf and grass, about 8 feet high and 20 yards square, into which a small wall has been built carrying a plaque with a brief statement in French recording the facts of the battle. The road along the ridge today runs precisely along the line of the 1346 road, past the mill. The bricks and flints of the original structure lie just beneath the surface of the mound, the view from which covers the whole field from Wadicourt round over the two low ridges, and then southwards over the ground where the Black Prince fought to the town of Crécy itself.

On the eastern side of the Val aux Clercs one may see, after ploughing and before the new corn has any height, a broad smear of white chalk, faint yet definite on the brown of the top soil. From nearby it cannot be seen, like the trench lines of 1916, and it is necessary to get several hundred yards away on some eminence in order to spot it. This smear at Crécy is opposite the little re-entrant where the French King's last desperate effort was so roughly handled, and all round is the ground where the charging French cavalry ran into the English archers' fire. There is little doubt that it is the remains of the chalk that was turned up for the mass graves in which the English buried the enemy dead, and that many bones and pieces of metal accoutrements lie close below the surface, just deep enough to have escaped the ploughing of centuries.

Wadicourt is a tightly knit little village that obviously could have greatly impeded a flank attack. But only 300 yards beyond it is open country again, and it is easy to see how, had the leader of the little flank attack been bolder or had had a better eye for the country, he might well have turned the English lines.

The present owner and farmer of the land reports that visitors often come to Crécy asking for the battlefield, but quickly lose interest when they see no mill and no physical signs of the battle, thinking all is changed. In fact, Crécy is totally unchanged except for the collapse of the mill.

Every year thousands of motorists leave Boulogne and drive down the Route Nationale 1 for Paris, Italy, the Riviera or Spain. Near Montreuil they are within 6 miles of the village of Crécy, which may be reached by turning left from the main road along the N338. On entering the village they should turn left around the Place and drive up the hill. On their right they will find the grass-covered heap of rubble indicating the position of Edward III's mill. They need go no further. From its eminence the whole field of Crécy can be surveyed.

Recently a small circular table-panorama has been built on the top of the grass-covered mound. The arrows on the table are most helpful. From its centre rises a short flagstaff, from which was flying, on the author's last visit, a very tattered Tricolour and below it an equally dejected Union Jack.

3 Agincourt: 1415

SITE *Twenty-seven miles north of Abbeville, 12 miles north of Hesdin, on the N28.*
CONTESTANTS *The French army of 20,000 under the Constable of France, with the equally authoritative Duke of Orléans (Marshal of France), Boucicault and the Duc d'Albert, all exercising command. The result was matchless confusion. The English army under Henry V of 6,000 men.*
CASUALTIES *The French lost 8,000 men, including the Constable and the Dukes of Bar and Alençon, while the Duke of Orléans was captured. The English lost about 400, the large majority of whom were wounded; many of the wounded would sooner or later die through gangrene caused by ignorance of the need for antiseptic care and proper dressings.*

PRESENT ACCOMMODATION *As for Crécy.*

Henry V's expedition to France in 1415 was made to reclaim his inheritance of those great areas in south-western France around Bordeaux, which had been lost as the Hundred Years War had progressed. His army consisted of 10,000 men and 25,000 horses, who embarked at Southampton, where the ships, none of more than 500 tons, lay alongside the jetties. Embarkation took two weeks, and each ship, when loaded, pulled out into the Solent or Spithead and anchored. When embarkation was complete, the fleet waited four days for a favourable wind, so that the earlier ships to load had to spend eighteen days at anchor, waiting – and rolling. The voyage across the Channel took three days, and on arrival the army landed on an open beach – where the docks of Le Havre now stand.

After their prolonged period on board the small troopships, in appalling discomfort, the men were very 'soft', not up to the hard work that was immediately required of them. They had to unload wagons, horses and stores from ships, while frequently getting wet, and then lead off wagons and pack-animals, in addition to pitching tents and the vast marquees for Henry and his court, which overtaxed their already lowered stamina. The weather was very hot, the men could not be prevented from eating all the fruit they could find or drinking the unaccustomed wine, and dysentery soon appeared.

By early October, when Henry had captured Harfleur and was ready to advance, his army had been greatly reduced by sickness. Realising that he could not now contemplate a deep advance into France, he contented himself with a semi-marauding expedition eastwards from Harfleur, intending to cross the Somme and make for Calais.

As Henry marched his army, now reduced to about 7,000 men, eastward, many men must have fallen out. Those barely convalescent from dysentery, those sickening for it, and the daily accident toll that is inevitable among an army on the march, were carried on the already overloaded wagons. The discomfort of a sick or injured man on a crude vehicle with primitive springs on rough roads must have been acute. Those who were too ill to be moved were left behind in religious houses, where 'sanctuary' was claimed. Outside these walls the stragglers from the invading army had short shrift from the peasants.

The sick men left behind could hope for no pay, or outside help at all, and on recovery could only give their labour in return for their keep. Most of the men left in 'sanctuary' were never rescued, France and England being in a state of semi-war for another thirty-six years, and it is probable that the blood of some of them now runs in the veins of villagers in Artois and Picardy.

In those days the news of the approach of an army of 7,000 men or so must have been received with dismay by villages or even small towns. The army, however friendly, would naturally consume vast stocks of food, forage, clothing, leather, wheels and harness; vehicles would be impounded to replace breakages or losses, but the King's 'treasurers' would not be very generous in paying them. Towns must have been stripped bare, and although the shopkeepers and alehouses did well, most people were glad to see the army march on.

The peasant population was naturally hostile to an invading army from a traditionally enemy country. Nevertheless, the British soldier was, in 1415, as adept at making friends with foreign civilians, especially the girls, as he was in 1914, and the local alehouses were crammed in the evenings with thirsty archers and men-at-arms who had a little pay to spend. Doubtless the enemy gained from 'careless talk' information as to movements, strengths of formations and morale, though the very limited knowledge and almost non-existent education of the men in the ranks could probably not give much away.

Henry's march from Harfleur up the Somme to Peronne, then back again along the north bank via Agincourt to Calais – 250 miles in twenty days – was one of the great marches in history. He crossed the Ancre at Miraumont and moved towards the villages of Agincourt, Tramecourt and Maisoncelles. Shortly after leaving Miraumont the army passed over the battlefield of Beaumont Hamel, to be fought over on 1 July 1916 at the start of the Battle of the Somme.

On reaching Maisoncelles, Henry halted his army for a night's rest. In the thickly wooded country all round him he realised that manoeuvre by the French was unlikely, and that they would almost certainly have to attack him frontally. Accordingly he ordered his archers to cut themselves wooden stakes from the woods, to be used as a form of breastwork.

Next day he moved on from Maisoncelles and took up a defensive position between the villages, and woods, of Agincourt and Tramecourt. The archers planted their spiked stakes in the soft ground, the flanks were secured by the woods and, as usual, the English stood on defence against attack by a continental army.

The first tactical move, a frontal attack by French cavalry, was easily repulsed by the English archers, the speed of the attack being greatly slowed by the heavy mud, for it had rained all night. This first assault was followed by a similar advance by French men-at-arms, but it too failed. Shot to pieces by the English arrows, it was also thrown into further confusion by the retreating cavalry from the first attack. The numbers of this second wave, however, were so great that the defending archers could not fire fast enough to stop them all, and a number of them breached the English line, where they were taken prisoner. The dead and wounded, together with the fallen horses from the first attack, made a vast pile of bodies, forming a secondary obstacle out in front. Henry ordered the archers from both flanks to wheel inward and shoot at the mass of bodies, some of whom were still alive. The armour of

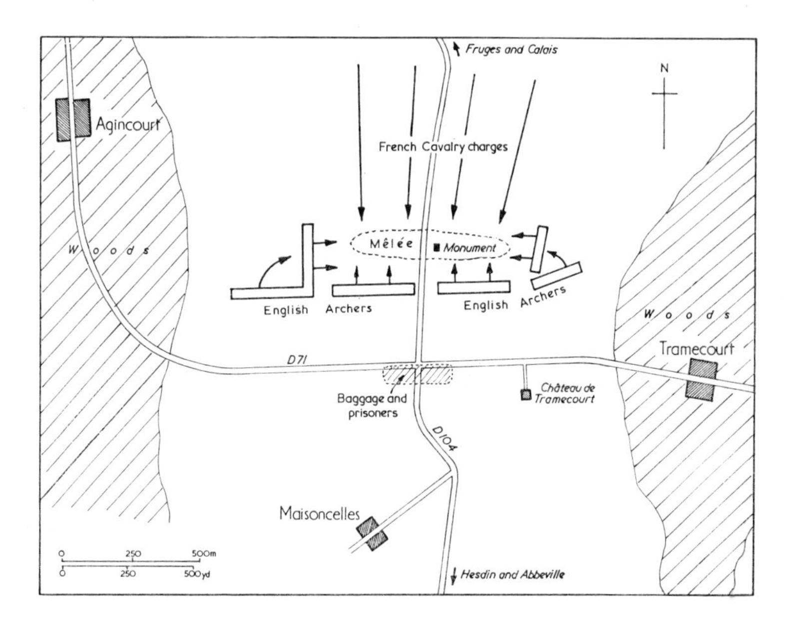

the French horsemen in that pile was so heavy that, when thrown from their horses, they could not get up without help, and the English men-at-arms, advancing through the archers, were able to kill them as the lay on the ground helpless and often unwounded.

The last French attack came from their cavalry reserve. Henry, knowing the exhaustion of his men and fearing an attack on them from the rear by his numerous French prisoners, gave his notorious order to kill them and so avoid simultaneous frontal and rearguard attacks. The last French attack did not come to much, however, and the remnant of the French army dispersed as best it could. Overcrowding both in the foot and mounted ranks, carrying too heavy armour, faced with efficient English archery, and impeded by heavy mud, the French suffered as great a defeat as at Crécy sixty-nine years previously. As at that battle, the English line did not move from its original position, apart from the inward wheel of the flank archers.

With the exception of the two woods of Agincourt and Tramecourt, about 2 miles apart, no physical features on this battlefield affected the action. It is a good tactical position and the advancing enemy were in full view for over a mile. The wood on Henry's left, which included the village of Agincourt, and Tramecourt Wood on the right both extend to the rear sufficiently to protect the wagons and rearward services.

On the Tramecourt side of the road bisecting the battlefield is a large crucifix, erected in 1870 by the then Vicomte de Tramecourt and his wife. It is in memory of the French soldiers who 'Set such a high standard of bravery and unselfishness in defending their country in 1415'.

Just outside the village of Tramecourt (which is nearer the battlefield than is Agincourt itself) is a magnificent eighteenth-century château, the home of the present Vicomte de Tramecourt. Inside the grounds and by the drive up to the château is another memorial, to the late Vicomte who died in captivity in 1945, aged fifty-five, and to his two sons, aged twenty-five and twenty, who also 'Died in captivity'. There is no other wording on the memorial.

On his first visit to Agincourt the author went back to see Maisoncelles and its horse-pond, where doubtless Henry watered his horses. Across the green came the village Curé, a charming cultured man. His very limited English and the author's even more limited French permitted communication, and a friendly chat ensued. After a while the Curé asked courteously the reason for this visit, and the author explained that he had come to visit and walk over the battlefield of Agincourt. At once the Curé's smile vanished, he bowed slightly, and, raising his hat, walked away.

The visitor to Agincourt from England should drive south from Calais to Montreuil, where a left turn leads to Hesdin, and left again there puts one on the road to Fruges. On the way the traveller will reach the village of Ruisseauville, where he should turn right for Maisoncelles. After about a mile, he will pass straight across the field of Agincourt, and if he stops at the great crucifix erected by the Vicomte de Tramecourt, he will be standing on the spot where Henry V's men inserted their stakes to resist the French cavalry charges. Another mile or so will take him into the village of Maisoncelles, where he will find the horse-pond.

4 Ramillies: 1706

SITE *Twenty-five miles south-east of Brussels, 25 miles west of Liège.*

CONTESTANTS

The Allies

7 British cavalry regiments	=	*3,500*
24 British infantry regiments	=	*19,500*
Danish cavalry and infantry	=	*7,000*
Dutch cavalry and infantry	=	*4,500*
		34,500 men and 120 guns

All under the Duke of Marlborough

The French

Cavalry	=	*4,500*
Infantry	=	*23,500*
		28,000 men and 70 guns

Under the command of Marshal Villeroi.

CASUALTIES *Allies killed or badly wounded, 3,600. French, from all causes, 18,000, of whom 6,000 were prisoners.*

LOSSES *The French lost fifty of their seventy guns, eighty sets of regimental colours and vast quantities of baggage.*

PRESENT ACCOMMODATION *At Namur, 15 miles south, Hôtel Porte de Fer is adequate. Nothing nearer is suitable. Brussels, 25 miles to the north-west, has hotels of every grade, of course.*

In 1706, two years after Blenheim, the second corner of Marlborough's Great Quadrilateral was fought at Ramillies. It is considered by many historians to come only second to Crécy as England's greatest victory over the French.

Marlborough, in Flanders with about 12,000 Dutch and Danish soldiers in addition to his own British army of 23,000, heard that the French army was about to move south towards Namur, and thereupon marched westward to anticipate the enemy near the village of Ramillies.

The French position there, of some strength on a high broad ridge facing east, had its southern boundary on the River Mehaign, with two villages, Taviers and Franquinay, forming the lower end of the ridge. Ramillies itself, in the centre and on the highest point was clearly of great importance while to its left the ground fell away again slowly into the considerable marsh in front of the village of Offuz.

About 1½ miles west of Taviers and also on high ground is a curiously shaped mound known as the Tomb of Ottomond. The main ridge, more particularly on its southern half and in front of Ramillies, slopes gradually down to the east for a 1,000 yards, and then flattens out.

Along the concave line of the villages, with Ramillies in the centre, the French were drawn up in two lines. Marlborough quickly realised that the French cavalry on the left, though entirely secured against attack by the marsh in front of them, were also incapable of aggressive action forward or round to its left for the same reason. Accordingly he opened his manoeuvres by a demonstration against the French left, sending forward a brigade of six British regiments against Offuz. Marching forward in full view, they crossed a low ridge and came down to the river and marsh to within a mile of the French. Here they seemed to be very busy in preparing their pontoons for crossing.

Villeroi, the enemy Commander-in-Chief, noted this mass of 'redcoats' and remembered from Blenheim that they were usually the vanguard at the main point of attack. Somewhat hastily he switched several battalions from his centre and right to reinforce his left. Having thus drawn these enemy reserves behind the marsh, Marlborough withdrew the six regiments to the ridge in their rear. Here the Buffs and Scots Fusiliers halted and turned about, crowning the rise with the scarlet line, and hiding the other four regiments, which rapidly marched off, unseen by the French.

The Buffs and Scots Fusiliers stood on the ridge all day without firing a shot, paralysing the whole of the French wing. The brigade commander had argued for a long while with the Staff Officer who brought the order to leave them there, and he only obeyed when Lord Cadogan, Marlborough's deputy, arrived to insist. Many of the men in these two regiments nursed a grievance for years, feeling that they had been denied their part in the battle.

Out on the Allied left flank about midday four Dutch battalions attacked Franquinay and Taviers, while twelve others, British and Dutch, advanced up the slope against Ramillies itself. Franquinay soon fell, but Taviers resisted for a long time, until a strong French reinforcement sent to its help was caught in flank and cut to pieces. The Dutch cavalry then pushed forward through this first gap in the enemy lines, but were repulsed by the second line. The situation on this extreme left flank becoming very confused.

Marlborough now led all the remaining Dutch and Danish cavalry into the mêlée. Recognised by some French dragoons in the middle of it, he was surrounded and his small escort almost overwhelmed. Unhorsed, he was in imminent danger of capture, when his ADC dismounted and gave him his horse. The escort rallied, encouraged by Marlborough's example under fire, and with him cut their way out of the confusion.

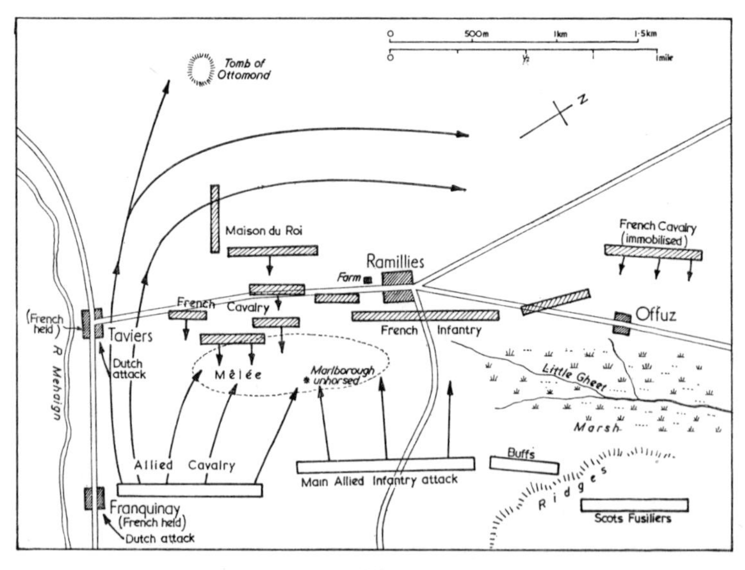

Meanwhile the main attack of British and Dutch infantry on Ramillies itself, advancing up the slopes, almost surrounded the village and entirely engaged the attention of the French and all their reserve cavalry. This pressure on the centre lessened the resistance of the French right, and the Danish cavalry and the Dutch Guards were able to move forward along the River Mehaign, outflanking the entire enemy right. The Dutch infantry swung round to their right, coming up behind the French line, while the Danish cavalry emerged on to the high ground by the Tomb of Ottomond. The famous Maison du Roi, the French regiment that had the honour to hold the right of the line, was cut to pieces, all the French cavalry between Ramillies and the river galloped off the field, and the remaining enemy infantry regiments were left helpless and alone.

Villeroi now tried to bring the unengaged cavalry from his left, to restore his right, but the marsh and the mass of his baggage train, left too far forward in the streets of Ramillies, greatly impeded them, and they were further hindered by French infantry beginning to give way in Ramillies. Marlborough now ordered the whole of the infantry massed before Ramillies to advance. The French centre in and around the village broke, and the enemy infantry streamed westward.

The 3rd and 6th Dragoon Guards, following the British and Dutch infantry into Ramillies, turned north, and passed behind those French troops still remaining behind the marsh. The Buffs and the Scots Fusiliers now marched forward down to the river, and, crossing the marsh, joined hands with the Dragoon Guards. The remaining elements of the French army all along the line then broke up in panic and fled.

The British cavalry being comparatively fresh quickly took up the pursuit. Ignoring the guns and baggage wagons they had captured and which they left to the infantry, they did not pause until far into the night, having covered fifteen miles. Nor was the main army far behind. Marching until 2 am they also captured many French infantry soldiers, the earlier deserters from Ramillies, as well as exhausted and horseless cavalrymen.

The French lost 18,000 men, of whom a third were prisoners, including a number who deserted during or after the action. Eighty sets of colours, fifty guns, and vast quantities of baggage were also captured in the fight. The Allies lost 3,600 men from all causes. These captures effectively disposed of the taunt levelled at Marlborough after Blenheim that he did not know how to 'improve' a victory.

Today the battlefield of Ramillies, 3 miles long, is difficult to see from one viewpoint, a fact that demonstrates the efficiency of Marlborough's subordinate commanders. His plan can only have been passed on in outline, largely composed of 'Intentions', and the divisional and brigade commanders obviously were experts in reading these intentions.

The only spot from where the whole field can be seen is within the French lines, where a large farmhouse, entirely rebuilt and now a modern building, stands at the southern end and at the highest point of the village of Ramillies. From its roof the British redcoats moving down to the Little Gheet and its marsh, and then withdrawing again to the ridge, must have been visible, although 1½ miles away. As Villeroi reacted so quickly to this move, it seems certain that his headquarters were at this farm.

The great barn of the farm is of much interest, for it has not been rebuilt. Two of the walls show the marks of Marlborough's cannon-balls, and the western end the scars of British machine-gun bullets fired at the German position around the farm just before the Armistice in 1918. In 1945 the straw-thatched roof was burnt off by an incendiary shell fired by the Herman Goering Division in its withdrawal. The walls have been raised a little and a new roof put on, but the fabric of the four main walls is untouched since 1706 except for the clearly visible repair work on the holes made by the cannon-balls.

Ramillies village itself is very compact and there seems to have been no expansion since 1706. Although none of the houses contemporary with the battle remain, the existing ones are clearly built on the old foundations, and the layout of the roads corresponds with those shown on early eighteenth-century maps. As a result it is possible to identify one's position very accurately – to see where the great cavalry mêlée took place, where Marlborough was unhorsed, where the Maison du Roi was crushed, and the slope up which the Dutch infantry advanced.

The villages of Offuz and Autre-Eglise clearly show that, with the marsh in front of them, they were almost unassailable, and that the French troops holding them were both secure and useless. The ridge on which the Buffs and Scots Fusiliers stood is, in fact, two ridges overlapping each other. Any movement on them must have been very obvious to the French.

The Tomb of Ottomond still stands, a most curious and incongruous feature alone in this gently rolling country. Sixty feet high and with a diameter of 100 yards, steep and covered with trees, it dominates the southern half of the battlefield. At first sight it looks like a barrow, enclosing the burial place of some important prehistoric royal personage. It is very similar to Silbury Hill on the Bath road near Avebury, but whereas at Silbury the ditch and pits from which the soil was excavated to build the hill can still be seen, here at Ramillies there are no signs at all of such excavations, and the entire absence of any signs of human labour in its erection suggest that it is in fact an extraordinary freak of nature.

Ramillies is easily found. Pass through the village of Taviers, where there is a signpost to Ramillies. The large building at the top of the hill on the left of the road is the great farmhouse where the marks of Marlborough's cannon-balls can still be seen.

In 1908 the grandfather of the present owner of the farm, when ploughing between Franquinay and Taviers, found the wheel of a cannon buried in a hedge. He carried it home and, sad to say, used it for firewood. In 1974 the author was given a musket bullet by the farmer-owner, picked up when ploughing recently.

5 Malplaquet: 1709

SITE *On the Mons–Le Cateau road 10 miles south of Mons, at the French–Belgian Frontier Customs Post.*
CONTESTANTS *The French had 95,000 soldiers, with sixty guns, under Marshal Villars. The Allied British, German and Austrian forces, totalled 110,000, of whom 60 per cent were British, with 100 guns. All under the command of Marlborough, at the height of his military career and power.*
CASUALTIES *The Allies lost 24,000 killed or badly wounded, the large majority caused by Orange's abortive and unauthorised attack. The French, although defeated, lost fewer men, 12,000 falling. The total casualties of 36,000, about 17 per cent of the forces engaged, rendered Malplaquet the bloodiest battle in British military history before Le Cateau in 1914.*

PRESENT ACCOMMODATION *One or two hotels in Mons are adequate for one night, and taxis are available at the station. Valenciennes, 20 miles away, has similar facilities. Motoring roads are good but stretches of* pavé *still exist.*

The fourth corner of Marlborough's Great Quadrilateral, Malplaquet, was fought at the end of the 1709 campaign.

The French, refreshed and reinforced after their third defeat in four years, at Oudenarde in 1708, were fearing an invasion from the north-east. To protect Arras, the north-eastern gate of France, they built a strong line of entrenchments facing the Low Countries, from La Bassée to south of Mons. The only undefeated French general, Marshal Villars, was in command.

Marlborough decided to move southward through a gap between

the woods of Lanières and Sars (Bois de Lanières and Bois de Sars), and there attack the great French entrenchments.

On the evening of 29 August the French were holding their lines in strength, with outposts in front, Marlborough was in bivouac around the village of Sars-la-Bruyères, about 4 miles away to the north.

Three rows of new trenches joined the two woods of Lanières and Sars at the narrowed point of the gap, about 1½ miles wide. The inner sides of the two woods, facing inwards across the gap, were roughly parallel. The woods were by no means impenetrable, and formed excellent cover for any flanking movements. Lanières Wood was three quarters of a mile long, and Sars straggled far out to the west. The French position at Malplaquet was very similar to that of the English at Agincourt of 1415. Henry V had had both flanks resting on thick woods impassable to cavalry, with his main defensive position well down the funnel.

The French held the triple line of trenches in great strength, while the inner sides of the two woods were held for some distance forward by units facing inwards towards each other. Detachments in some rear trenches behind the main position guarded Malplaquet, and finally, in the rear of them all, stood the cavalry.

Two detachments of German and Austrian troops started the action for the Allies by attacking the northern and eastern faces of Sars Wood, on the left of the French position. The main British infantry were drawn up in the centre, ready to advance down the gap when their right flank had been guarded by the clearing of Sars Wood. A strong detachment under General Withers with nineteen battalions and two cavalry regiments moved far out to their right, to encircle Sars Wood and turn the extreme French left.

The attack on the eastern face of the wood proceeded well at first. The Austrians passed through marshes and streams as they neared the French position, but after a slight penetration were eventually held up by the fire from deep inside the wood. Extending their left, and in full deployment, they could make little further headway.

The Germans fared little better. Pressing into the northern point of the wood, they drove in French outposts and, later, some isolated enemy regiments, but they were also brought to a halt by the western end of the main trench line, held by Picardie, the senior French regiment of the line, which would not yield. Three British regiments – the Buffs, the Bedfords, and Temple's – were sent by Marlborough around the right but were met by an enemy counterattack. (Temple's Regiment had no other name. It was raised in 1702 and disbanded in 1713. Little is known of it.) Picardie at last fell back and the Germans and Austrians advanced again. The wood, however, becomes very dense at its southern end,

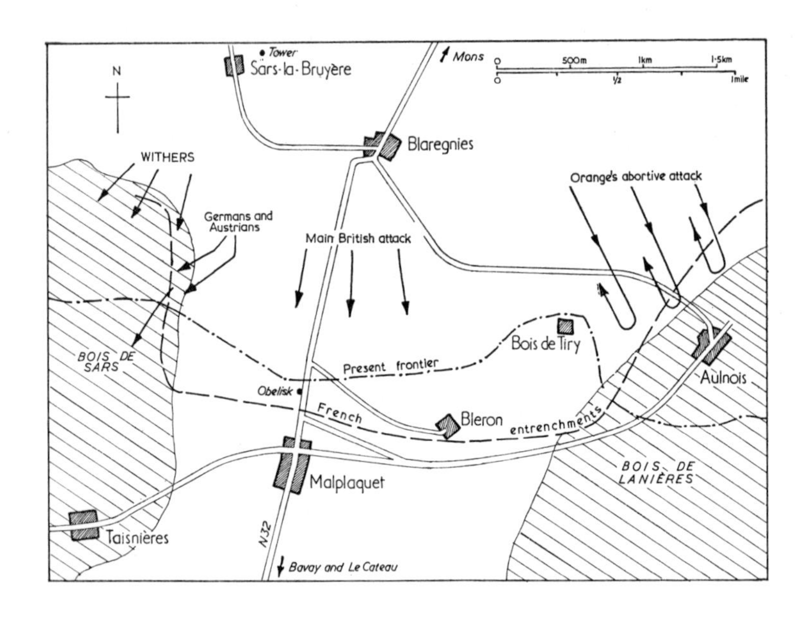

and all touch with neighbouring units was lost. French parties left behind in the orderly withdrawal became mixed up with Germans, Austrians and British, and soon small bands of men, all sense of direction gone, were stalking each other in great confusion.

Tripping over felled trees, forcing their way through thick undergrowth and bog, guided only by flashes of musket fire in front of them, the attackers nearly met Withers' extreme right flank movement. Villars, seeing the danger, rapidly moved several regiments from the main trench between the two woods to counterattack, at first successfully, but Withers arrived just when he was wanted. His advance through the wood had been led by the Royal

Irish (the 18th Foot), which met and repulsed the French Royal Regiment of Ireland.

Impatient at not being allowed to move while the Sars Wood battle was progressing, the Prince of Orange, commanding a large force on the Allied left, advanced without orders against the northern end of Lanières Wood. The trenches on the edge of this wood were well sited, and Orange's attack was greatly slowed by accurate French musket fire. Most of the Prince's staff were shot, as was his horse. Nevertheless he continued to lead his men on foot until they came within range of artillery on their left flank. This caused further heavy casualties but they continued their advance and finally reached the wood. A counterattack, however, drove them back. Six thousand men were killed in this unauthorised operation, and Orange's precipitation had brought about little less than a disaster, badly upsetting Marlborough's battle plan.

When stalemate in the Sars Wood battle was reached, Marlborough moved a forty-gun battery down the gap between the two woods to within range of the main line of trenches. After a heavy bombardment, Lord Orkney led the main British infantry division through and round the guns and assaulted the enemy's main position, capturing it at the first advance, though with considerable losses. Cavalry passed through and attacked the still stubbornly resisting French infantry in their third line, now some hundreds of yards behind their original position, and in front of Malplaquet village.

Villars, who had been badly wounded, was succeeded by his second-in-command, old Boufflers, a French general called from retirement. Boufflers recognised defeat when he saw it, and ordered a general withdrawal.

The Great Quadrilateral had been completed. Four times in six years Marlborough had attacked and beaten the great French army led by experienced generals. His fame, as a general who never lost a battle, had been assured.

The French withdrawal was admirably conducted, as the French, though beaten, were not routed, and the Allies were too exhausted to pursue with any vigour. The French lost 12,000 men, 500 prisoners, fifty sets of colours and sixteen guns.

The Allied losses were far heavier. Twenty-four thousand

men were killed or wounded, largely due to the mad onset of the Prince of Orange. The Dutch lost more than half their number. The British lost 2,000 from twenty battalions.

The battlefield of Malplaquet is very flat, being mostly pasture. In order to keep the cattle and sheep within the bounds of their owners, fences with one or two strands of wire are plentiful everywhere. Most of the fence posts are unremarkable, but now and again a gnarled piece of tree is used, and it is likely that such posts as these were taken from the revetments of the great French trench. Doubtless the French soldiers in the thirty-six hours allowed them before the battle cut these posts from the woods of Sars and Lanières, and after the battle, when the armies had passed on, the local peasants salvaged them to re-erect the fences knocked down in the fighting. Similar adaptations are to be seen on the old 1914–18 front line in France and Belgium, where returning villagers in 1919 salvaged screw picquets, angle-irons and barbed wire from the trenches all round them for their cottage and farmstead enclosures, and corrugated iron from old dug-outs for pigsties.

At Malplaquet no trace of the line of the great trenches can be seen at all, but its approximate position can be fixed. It ran almost along the line of the present Franco–Belgian frontier, midway between the two modern customs posts (about 500 yards apart). Between them stands a large obelisk commemorating the Frenchmen killed in the battle. A large plaque on its front facing the road carries two cameo relief portraits of Villars and Boufflers, the former superimposed on the latter, and around the rim with their names the words 'Soldats de France'.

Here on the battlefield of Malplaquet, three days before the Armistice in November 1918, the advancing British army had a minor engagement with a retreating German rearguard. Three officers and five men of the Royal Warwicks, who were killed, are buried in the village cemetery, half a mile behind the battlefield of 1709.

The Bois de Sars is less changed in shape and condition than the Bois de Lanières. A mile long and about a quarter of a mile wide today, the eastern inner edge is the original. It is still very boggy, with dense undergrowth, and it is very easy to imagine how the British regiments, their sub-units particularly, lost their way as they advanced, and to be surprised that the French were able to withdraw in orderly fashion. Visibility is rarely more than 30 yards, and the smoke from musket fire, a feature of eighteenth- and nineteenth-century warfare unknown today, must have added greatly to the existing confusion.

At Sars-la-Bruyère, 4 miles to the north, is a large tower almost in a state of ruin. It was the keep of a medieval château, whose roof today gives a magnificent view of the battlefield. Marlborough surveyed the ground from there, and planned the battle and issued his orders in the one great room below. His descendant Sir Winston Churchill mounted the steep and narrow stairway to study the battlefield before writing his chapter on Malplaquet in his book *Life of Marlborough.*

In Bavai, 4 miles to the south, lives a retired judge, eighty years of age, whose grandfather picked up three circular lead bullets about half an inch in diameter on the battlefield. The old judge thinks that was around 1815.

6 Fontenoy: 1745

SITE *Sixteen miles east of Tournai, in Belgium, on the Tournai–Mons road, N61, and 2 miles south of Ramecroix.*
CONTESTANTS *An Allied army of 53,000, mostly British, with eighty guns, under the Duke of Cumberland, son of George II, opposed 70,000 French, with seventy guns, under Marshal Saxe.*
CASUALTIES *About 7,000 for each side. A narrow victory for the French.*

PRESENT ACCOMMODATION *Two or three very adequate hotels in Tournai and Lille. Mons not recommended. Roads good but* pavé *still exists in short lengths even on main roads.*

For 30 years after Malplaquet in 1709 France as a military power was much humbled while the national armies of Spain, Austria, Hanover, Bavaria and Prussia all took heart. In 1745, however, the coalition of the German states supporting Austria broke up, and the French, seeing their chance, invaded the Austrian Netherlands with an army of 80,000 under the command of the famous Marshal Saxe, one of France's most able generals ever. It was at once victorious, and succeeded in laying siege to the important fortified town of Tournai. A smaller force of the Allies advanced to the relief of Tournai under the command of the Duke of Cumberland, the victor of Culloden, eleven months later, where he earned the name of Butcher Cumberland.

Saxe's burden at Tournai was not lightened by the arrival in his camp of King Louis XV, and his son, the Dauphin, later to be Louis XVI and guillotined in 1794. Their arrival brought great encouragement to the men in the ranks and the junior officers, but they were a major embarrassment at Headquarters. Their retinue was enormous, including as it did chaplains, almoners, provosts, valets de chambre, barbers, tailors, cooks, surgeons, and even the royal clock winders. All had to be accommodated in proper style and dignity, which was difficult, but, worse than that, they provided many unproductive mouths to be fed from within the limited commissariat. In addition they provided many amateur tacticians who had the King's ear, and much ill-informed criticism of Saxe was fed to him. Lastly Saxe's burden included the safety of the Royal person. The possibility of Louis being captured would be more serious than his being killed in battle. Such a capture, though of little material loss to the country, would have been a staggering blow to the prestige of France and the mystique of the monarchy. But Saxe was a great man, as events were to show, and he carried his heavy burdens triumphantly.

Leaving some 20,000 men behind him to conduct the siege, he moved his main body out to the south-east of Tournai to meet the Allied army marching up from Mons. On his arrival near the village of Fontenoy, Saxe employed similar tactics to those he had seen used at Malplaquet thirty-three years before, when, as a Saxon, he had fought under Marlborough against the French. He rested his left on the village of Ramecroix and his right on the village of Fontenoy, while extending a strong right flank back at right-angles to the main line. Opposite the left of his main position was a large wood, the Bois de Barri, in the south-west corner of which he built two redoubts. He posted his Irish contingent of six battalions close up to the western face of the wood, behind some wooden breastworks, there to contain any British infantry who might debouch into open country again.

In the centre and on the right of the Irish contingent he placed seven battalions of French guards, who were to take the full weight of the Allied attack. Behind them were another six line battalions, as a reserve.

In the little village of Fontenoy many of the houses were turned into miniature fortresses, loopholes being knocked in the walls and windows sandbagged. On the little grass-covered village square trenches were dug.

Both wings now secure, the main position had the added

advantage of being on top of a gentle slope, which the enemy would have to climb in the face of the musketry of the French guards. Neatly bisecting the battlefield ran an important road, running westward to Tournai. About a mile behind Saxe's last line of reserves stood the small hamlet of Notre Dame des Bois. Here the King, Dauphin and several court officials took up their position.

Cumberland was only twenty-three and of course very inexperienced. Indeed, his only qualification for supreme command was that he had fought bravely at Dettingen, though princely rank enabled him to impose something like unity on his subordinates.

On 8 May his army, after an exhausting 50-mile cross-country march, had reached the villages 2 miles to the east of Fontenoy. Here, in Wasmes, Maubray and Vezon, they enjoyed a two-day rest after their gruelling march.

In the afternoon of 10 May the Allies moved out from their rest camps, driving off some French outposts in front of them, and entered the Bois de Barri. Here Saxe had posted numerous irregulars, little more than untrained local foresters who were good shots and whose orders were to withdraw, fighting, to the west, disorganising the British advance in the process and luring it on to the two redoubts.

Throughout the night there was chaos in the wood, and although casualties on both sides were minimal, much energy was expended, accompanied by frustration. However, at midnight Cumberland made plans for a grand assault at dawn.

On the right a newly formed brigade consisting of the Suffolks, Somerset Light Infantry, Black Watch, and a Hanovarian regiment, was to attack through the wood against the redoubt, while on the left the Dutch would strike against the village of Fontenoy. A massive attack in the centre was to follow.

The attack on the two redoubts failed miserably. The defending irregulars in the wood continued to delay the advancing infantry, and those men who did penetrate so far as to be within musket shot of the redoubts were met with a biting fire and pinned to their ground. Cumberland galloped up and, cursing the brigade commander volubly in fluent German and broken English, ordered him to advance again. The soldiers saw that to try to pass between the two redoubts, or anywhere near them, was extremely hazardous. They refused to move, remaining inactive for several hours. For three such excellent regiments and one other to refuse to advance against the enemy because of the danger seems a most remarkable circumstance, surely without parallel in British military history. Not only did the regiments refuse to advance but their brigade commander, Ingoldsby, although ordered by Cumberland in the presence of the men to do so, refused as well. Cumberland's fury is both understandable and justified.

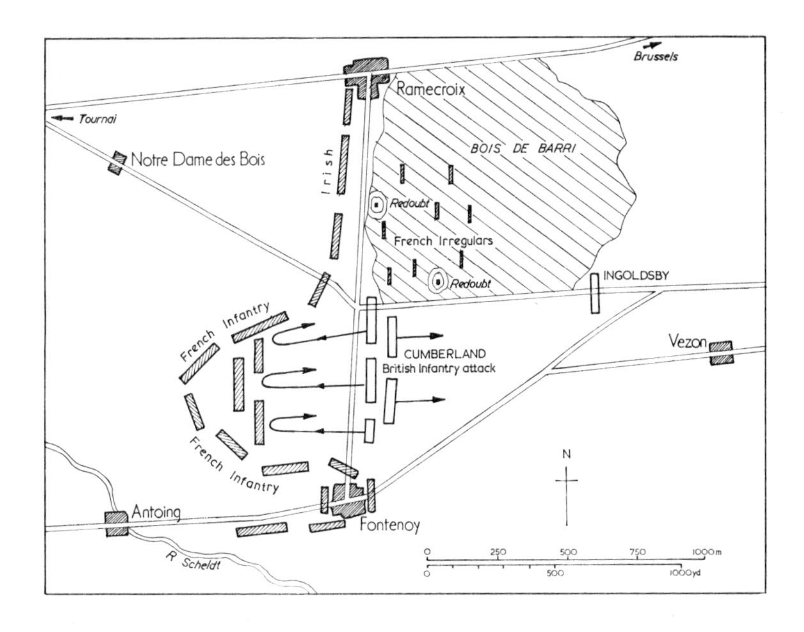

British regiments have turned and run in panic more than once, but only at Fontenoy can it be recalled that danger alone led the men to disobey orders. It cannot have been lack of morale caused by extreme fatigue, for the men had enjoyed two nights' sleep, and usually one night's sleep after a great effort rejuvenates young and fit men. It could have been genuine bad discipline in one regiment, but that is unlikely to be found in two battalions in a brigade only formed the previous day, while for three of them to be so effected seemed wildly improbable. Perhaps Ingoldsby was extremely unpopular for some reason, though there is no evidence of this, and such dislike could hardly have developed in the few hours since he had taken over the newly formed brigade.

The remaining possibility is that Ingoldsby himself was not only afraid of the French but also of his own men. Apparently this fear was strong enough for him to stand up to Cumberland's anger, and it is remarkable that Cumberland did not immediately relieve him of his command, replacing him not with one of the COs of the recalcitrant battalions but by a senior officer from elsewhere. Later in the day Ingoldsby was wounded, and after the battle he was court-martialled for disobeying orders, but there is no evidence of the findings of the court. However, Cumberland gave him three months in which to leave the army. Had the incident occurred in 1943 at El Alamein, Ingoldsby would have been given three minutes in which to leave the army.

On the left of the Allies' advance things were little better. An enveloping attack was tried against the embattled village of Fontenoy by eight battalions, but it failed, with the loss of 1,500 men. Cumberland was undaunted, however, and decided to attack in force in the centre and to smash his way through. A magnificent feat of arms followed.

Seventeen British battalions, ten in the front rank, followed by seven others, advanced up the slope between the south-west corner of the Bois de Barri and the northernmost houses of Fontenoy village. On the right of the advance was the Guards Brigade of three battalions, the Grenadiers being, of course, on the right of the line. Next to the Guards came the Royal Scots, Scots Fusiliers, East Surreys, the King's Own Scottish Borderers (KOSB), the Duke of Wellington's Regiment (the Dukes), and on the left of the line the Green Howards.

The French artillery tore great gaps in the British ranks, but they could not be stopped. Since the French front lay in a broad shallow re-entrant, the ten battalions in the front of the British advance were gradually compressed together until, moving up this funnel of fire, there was room for only six of them, an open target for the French guns. The British ranks were closed time and again as they came on.

They crossed over the Fontenoy–Ramecroix road and eventually halted only 40 yards from the French Guards. The Colonel of the Grenadiers, Lord Charles Hay, took out his silver hip-flask, bowed to the French officers, drank with ostentation, and called out: 'I hope, gentlemen, that you will not run away as you did at Dettingen.' One of Hay's sergeants then shouted: 'For what we are about to receive may the Lord make us truly thankful.' From these two anecdotes sprang the legend that a British junior officer called out in his turn: 'Will the gentlemen of the French Guard be pleased to fire first.' There is no evidence that these words, or anything comparable, were ever uttered.

As the great line of advance halted, the French riflemen opened fire, though raggedly and ineffectively. Doubtless they were awed by the scarlet-coated troops whom they could not halt and whose ranks were now so close. At last the British regiments could fire, and they opened up volley after volley. The majority of the front rank of the French Guards dropped, and despite reserves brought up to plug the gaps, the enemy line wavered and almost disintegrated.

The British continued their advance for another 300 yards into the heart of the French position, by Saxe's headquarters, and it seemed the Allies had won the day. King Louis, his son, and their entourage were strongly advised to withdraw, but they had now become an asset to Marshal Saxe. The blow to the morale of the French infantry, never high in defence, might have been shattering if they had retired. Saxe insisted on their remaining.

The tactical position was now excellent for the British and equally disastrous for the French, whose centre was almost pierced. But the salient into the French main position was narrow and the victorious British units perforce much crowded. The enemy flanks were holding, and their guns behind the Bois de Barri and in Fontenoy village turned their fire on the redcoats. This fire, together with small-arms fire from the French flanks caught the British in enfilade, causing heavy losses. Now was the time for the two Allied wings to advance and take the pressure off the harassed front-line units.

Cumberland could see a mass of French cavalry forming up in front of his previously successful advance, presumably to act as a screen for the shattered French Guards. To meet the anticipated cavalry charge the British formed not into square but oblong. This was a new formation, with six battalions in front, six in rear and three facing outwards.

By now the fight was at a standstill, with no movement beyond the exchange of guns and musket fire. But Saxe was well aware that one or both of his flanks might collapse, and that the longer the fire fight went on, the greater the danger of the successful British advance in the centre being resumed. He therefore ordered forward all those French regiments that had retained some steadiness and cohesion, and they nearly surrounded the almost isolated British mass. Cumberland, realising the danger of this isolation, ordered a methodical withdrawal. The British regiments had now been on their feet, advancing, firing and fighting, for eight hours. Despite heavy losses in their advance, they thought they had won a great victory. Their chagrin at now having to retreat was acute. Nevertheless, without confusion or wavering, they turned and marched steadily down the rise. Every 100 yards they turned and delivered one of their paralysing volleys, while the cavalry, the Blues much to the fore, galloped around harassing the rather disorganised advances of the French. The British reached the shelter of the Bois de Barri and the villages, bloody but unbowed.

This was the time for counterstroke by the French, for which there was plenty of French cavalry available. But Saxe did nothing, and the retiring British infantry was allowed to get away. Later he said that he knew the British cavalry was comparatively intact, spoiling for a fight, and would be eager to screen their infantry brothers after their defeat. He also suspected, rightly, that the British had a hidden reserve, including some of the formidable Highlanders. The British army was allowed to march away into the night.

The total of Allied killed and wounded amounted to 7,000, The French, on the defensive until the last hour, lost at least a similar number, and the hospitals of Lille, Douai, Cambrai and Valenciennes were filled for months afterwards.

The battlefield of Fontenoy is both disappointing and interesting. The main area where the British advance and withdrawal took place is now one vast area of enormous cornfields, with no hedges, cottages or paths to indicate one's whereabouts. The Bois du Barri has been cut back, and its western edge, the nearest to the battlefield, is now half a mile away. The two redoubts have disappeared under the plough. Right across the battlefield and probably about when the British advance was finally halted runs a broad two-way motor road. Standing on the embankments above the road, one can hope that one is near the centre of the action, no more.

The village green in Fontenoy village, a very rare feature in Belgian of French villages, is worth visiting. About 800 yards square, it is surrounded by old cottages, doubtless built on the foundations of the 1745 buildings, the comparatively modern church, and one very old barn. This barn was probably standing in 1745, and the annual coats of whitewash, so beloved of Belgian farmers, probably hide the scars of the loopholes knocked in the walls. In the centre of the village green stands an impressive memorial to the battle in general and the Irish troops serving in Louis XV's army in particular. These excellent soldiers held the French left flank, and although pressed back by the Guards, formed a strong and dependable wing.

The memorial, erected in 1874 by the Irish Military Historical Society of Dublin, was designed by an Irish architect and raised by an Irish builder. On the outer wall of the little cemetery further up the road, on the outskirts of the village, are two further plaques to the memory of the Irish soldiers.

7 Valmy: 1792

SITE *One mile north of the main N3, Paris-Châlons-Verdun-Metz, at Orbeval, 20 miles east of Châlons.*

CONTESTANTS *The French Revolutionary army comprised 25,000 men with forty guns under old Kellerman, plus late reinforcements from Dumouriez. The Allies, mostly Prussians, but including Austrians and 15,000 young French 'Aristos', totalled 120,000, with thirty-six guns. They were commanded by King Frederick William II of Prussia and the Duke of Brunswick.*

CASUALTIES *The Prussians lost 1,200 killed and wounded, and the French only 350, most of which came from artillery fire while they were standing in their ranks. These casualties are trivial compared with the numbers engaged, and the great importance of Valmy emerges in the text.*

PRESENT ACCOMMODATION *Hotels in Châlons, 20 miles, and Verdun, 30 miles, are excellent. The roads are superb and the whole sparsely populated area is delightful country.*

The French Revolution of 1789 was not so much a revolution against the monarchy or the government as against excessive privilege.

In France there was no middle class. Instead the country was divided between the upper and lower classes. A very small minority of rich aristocrats, who received preferential tax treatment, sometimes paying none at all, were the only Frenchmen to be acceptable at court, and the only ones with a chance of securing government appointments. The vast majority of the people lacked these privileges, being taxed up to the hilt and denied a vote. Worst of all, they had to pay tribute from their farm produce to the court and the great nobles on whose lands they lived, and from which they scratched a bare living.

In 1790 the Paris mob rose and marched to Versailles, whence they forcibly removed the monarch, Louis XVI, his family, and the leading members of the court to the Tuileries, where Louis no longer ruled, although he precariously retained his throne.

Contrary to English public belief, Louis was quite popular. He was the fourth Louis in succession, his two immediate predecessors had ruled France for 130 years, his very name implied continuity and security and the Paris mob regarded him as a father figure. They believed he would prevent the Revolutionary extremists from going too far, and that while he was in Tuileries, although with little power, everything would be all right.

Then Louis took a disastrous step. He, with his immediate family, tried to escape, but were captured and brought back to Paris. His escape route to the east led directly towards the frontier between France and the Holy Roman Empire, behind which stood the armies of Austria and Prussia. At once all Frenchmen realised that he had gone to make common cause with France's enemies, and, had he reached the frontier and safety, would probably have led the Allies against them. His popularity disappeared overnight; everyone believed that not only was he an enemy of the newly formed Revolutionary society and system but he was also an enemy of France. From that moment he was doomed.

At the end of September 1792 Dumouriez, commanding a French Revolutionary army of 20,000 men, was operating in the northern reaches of the Argonne, while Kellerman, commanding another Revolutionary army of 25,000 men, was near Metz, some 40 miles to the east.

The Allied army consisted of 60,000 Prussians, 45,000 Austrians, and, most important of all, 15,000 Frenchmen, a total of 120,000 men. The Frenchmen were the younger sons of families uprooted by the Revolution. Many were young aristocrats trained to arms from childhood. They looked upon the road to Paris, along which they would carve history, as the road to honour, the rescue of their King, reunion with their families and estates and finally, but very importantly, the restoration of their nobility and the privileges it brought. In command of this imposing and highly trained force the allied sovereigns had placed the Duke of Brunswick, an able man who in the Seven Years War as a pupil of Frederick the Great had learned his trade in a hard but excellent school.

Dumouriez was holding the defiles of the Argonne as a screen against the Allies to allow Kellerman to advance eastward beyond Metz; but an apparently unimportant pass had been left unguarded and an Austrian corps slipped through, seriously threatening Dumouriez's outer flank and rear. No alternative but immediate withdrawal remained, and Dumouriez's untrained troops, many of whom deserted, streamed back in disorder.

Kellerman, hearing the bad news from Dumouriez, halted his advance, unwilling to move into territory held by a vastly superior force of the enemy with the support on his left now in jeopardy. He started to withdraw but was asked by Dumouriez to stand on the high ground near Ste Menehould where he, Dumouriez, would join forces with him, and altogether they would bar the road to Paris from Verdun.

On the evening of 19 September two staff officers rode in from Dumouriez's headquarters to tell Kellerman that the Allies were wheeling southward and occupying high ground to his west, and were in fact between him and Paris. Evidently Brunswick, commanding the Allied army, felt he dare not move on the capital while both Kellerman's and Dumouriez's forces remained in his rear, and that he must defeat them first.

Kellerman deployed his 25,000 men on the high ground 6 miles west of Ste Menehould around a windmill that stood on the highest point. Dumouriez was still some distance away, but, realising his comrade's dangerous and exposed position, sent forward by forced march some of his best troops in support.

Kellerman's force held a convex position around the mill. The right flank, bent sharply back, overlooked the village of Valmy, 600 yards from the mill, and the withdrawn left flank, facing south, overlooked a broad, gently sloping valley. The main strength of the army lay along the highest part of the plateau, the forward units about 200 yards out in front of the windmill, and the rear ones along the line where the little chapel and the car park stand today. The extreme Allied left wing stood in front of the hamlet of Somme-Dionne, lining the almost flat crest of the high ground and squarely faced Kellerman at the mill.

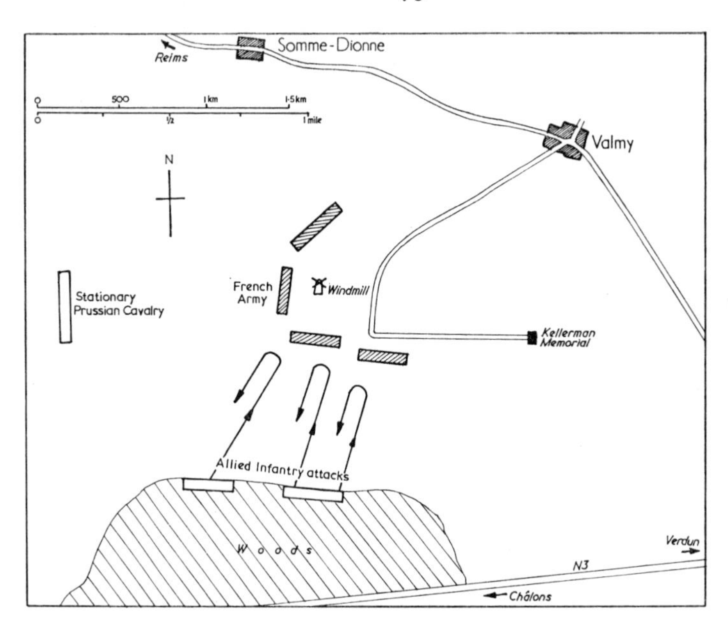

The Prussian cavalry along the broad ridge in front of the mill and 600 yards away must have been a magnificent sight. The breastplates, accoutrements and well-groomed horses catching the sun's rays may well have struck terror into the hearts of ill-trained infantry standing to receive them. The ground across which the cavalry could have charged remains as it was in 1792, and, being September, the corn had been cut, leaving no obstacles in the cavalry's path.

The woods to the south-west shielded any movement there, but immediately any troops debouched therefrom they came into full view from the mill. An advance from this quarter led downhill initially, but then had to cross open level ground before ascending the rise. Along the front edges of these woods lay the Allied batteries, whose fire on the French lines around and on top of the windmill crest was accurate, causing some casualties.

Contrary to the expectations of both sides, the French Revolutionary infantry held their ground, showing no signs of wavering, and their artillery replied, considerably neutralising some of the Allied guns and causing casualties to their massed infantry. Indeed Kellerman, believing that the enemy's fire was slackening, formed an assault column of infantry and led it in person down the slope into the valley, hoping to capture some of the foremost enemy guns. But a hidden battery opened up on the charging column, driving it back and killing Kellerman's horse under him. Unseated, he was in great danger of capture and was rescued with difficulty.

Seeing the repulse of the French sortie, the Allied infantry columns advanced from their cover in the woods and began a great attack across the valley against the French. Although they presented magnificent targets, which at 700 yards could hardly be missed. the French gunners had been shaken by the repulse of Kellerman's sorties, and began to waver, many leaving their guns. A complete collapse of the defence, which in that open country so much depended on artillery, seemed possible, but Kellerman again came to the front. Posting himself in the foremost rank of the infantry battalion likely to be attacked first he called on the men to stand with him, to let the enemy come close and then charge, at his orders, with the bayonet. His example of bravery, steadfastness, and patriotism became infectious and spread along the line, the men calling out 'Vive la Nation'.

The attacking enemy was now about to ascend the not very steep slope, but seeing the apparently immovable and resolute lines of Frenchmen, and hearing the shouting, they in their turn also wavered. They paused for some time in the valley, no man moving, no one seeming to be in command on the spot, no mounted officer exhorting them to advance. Then slowly, and still in formation, the Allies withdrew up their side of the valley and disappeared into the woods.

The King of Prussia bitterly reproached his normally steady soldiers for withdrawing in face of such an enemy, and called for another advance which he would lead in person. But the French artillery, now greatly heartened by their success against the first Allied attack, opened fire again. The French line at the mill was now also extended and thickened by the arrival of Dumouriez's reinforcements. The attack petered out and, leaving 800 dead behind them, the Allies left the field.

The numerically weaker French army remained victorious on the heights of Valmy, not knowing whether they would again be attacked or that in a few hours they had made history. Their victory had removed the great threat to the young French Revolution. By their steadfastness they had made the Allies doubt their ability to overthrow the Revolution by force. The chance now to replace Louis XVI on his throne had disappeared. The French had also shown the world, and history, the importance of morale. A numerically inferior and ill-trained army whose men were burning with enthusiasm for their revolution – a revolution that had released them, they thought, from tyranny and for which they would fight to the death – had proved more than a match for a larger army that had lacked these indefinable psychological spurs.

The Duke of Brunswick's great army wasted away in the hills and woods of the Argonne, where lowered morale was aggravated by sickness, and finally only a fraction recrossed the frontier. Marathon and Valmy are comparable. In each case a numerically inferior army with a 'cause' was to triumph over its apparently stronger enemy.

The whole of the battlefield can be seen from one central viewpoint – the windmill. The broad ridge along which the Prussian cavalry could, and should, have charged is very apparent. The wood sheltering the Allied guns and infantry are unchanged. The valley they essayed to cross is under the plough, and the drop into it from the windmill plateau is very slight.

Running back from the highest point at the windmill and at right-angles to it is another broad ridge. At its eastern end, about 400 yards from the mill, is a great statue to Kellerman in his revolutionary military uniform. Around the base of the statue, which is 20 feet high, stand twelve muzzle-loading cannon barrels, each mounted on a little concrete pillar. They are identical and are all stamped 'Joseph Whitworth & Co., Manchester, 1170 lbs.' They are all numbered, but, surprisingly, not consecutively, the twelve numbers running from 795 to 875. Presumably they were ordered by the French government from Whitworth's before the Revolution and were commandeered by those parts of the army that went over to the insurgents.

An hour is sufficient to see this battlefield. The only two points to visit are the enormous and much-restored windmill, and old Kellerman's statue and gun barrels. The car park is less than 200 yards from the windmill, and direction posts in the village of Valmy are helpful.

Were it not for its notoriety as a 'decisive battle of the world', Valmy from an historical tactical aspect is not very interesting.

However, in view of the result of the battle, it demands a visit. The military features of the action are almost negligible, there are no tactical moves to consider, and there are no physical features that influenced those tactics. The French defence was never really tested, and the only noteworthy circumstances was the complete futility of the Allies.

8 Quatre Bras: 1815

SITE *The Quatre Bras (The Four Arms) crossroads, 20 miles south of Brussels on the Charleroi road, and 8 miles south of Waterloo, also on the Charleroi road, N5.*
CONTESTANTS *The Allies, under Wellington, totalled 36,000 men, of whom 12,000 were British, the balance being Dutch, Belgian and German. The French army, under Ney, had 20,000 men. About one-tenth of each force was cavalry.*
CASUALTIES *The Allies lost 4,700 killed and wounded, and Ney lost 4,300.*

PRESENT ACCOMMODATION *Hotels in Brussels, Namur and Mons, which are equidistant from the battlefield.*

In October 1814 the Congress of Vienna assembled to settle the national boundaries disrupted by Napoleon's nineteen years of war. On 7 March 1815, when the Congress was about to adjourn for four months, word reached it that Napoleon had left Elba, presumably for France. Wellington was at once appointed Commander-in Chief of all the British, Dutch, Belgian and Hanovarian troops in the Low Countries.

Napoleon knew that he must move fast before the concentration against him could become effective. By superhuman efforts he reorganised in Paris what was left of the Grand Army after his abdication; enlisted 400,000 recruits, and fed, clothed, equipped and armed them all; and marched up to the north-east corner of France. This staggering piece of administration took eighty-five days.

The majority of the new French army were recruits. Most of the old soldiers from the Peninsular and Russian campaigns were transferred to the Guards. The army was very uneven in its quality, training, experience and discipline, but was bound together by enthusiasm for its brilliant leader and by the glory of 'La Grande Armée'.

Active operations in the Waterloo campaign began in the early hours of 15 June 1815, when the French crossed the Sambre and attacked the Prussians, and ended in the early hours of the 19th. In these ninety-six hours three great battles were fought, some 11,000 Allied and French soldiers lost their lives, and Napoleon, the colossus of Europe and perhaps the greatest captain in history, was irrecoverably overthrown. The British infantry in their squares became a legend. In ninety-six hours Great Britain and Europe passed from mortal danger to the beginning of ninety-nine years of safety.

The Allies under Wellington were billeted around Brussels, and in neighbouring towns. Of the 36,000 infantrymen, cavalrymen and artillerymen under Wellington's command, approximately one-third were British and two-thirds German, Dutch and Belgian.

On the evening of 15 June Napoleon attacked the Prussians at Ligny. Forced back with heavy casualties, the Prussians withdrew in the darkness, not north-east to their lines of communication, as anticipated by Napoleon, but north and then north-west to maintain touch with Wellington.

Before attacking the Prussians Napoleon prudently detached two corps under Generel Ney to contain the British army and its Allies under Wellington. Ney's orders were to force Wellington to remain on the defensive and so prevent him from moving to the help of old Blücher at Ligny. Wellington was to be gripped by Ney, Napoleon's left hand, while his right smashed the Prussians.

On the evening of 15 June, while Wellington and many of his officers were attending the Duchess of Richmond's famous ball in Brussels, he heard that Napoleon had advanced against the Prussians. Immediately he ordered Picton's Division of British infantry to march out to Quatre Bras, an important crossroads 20 miles south of Brussels, 10 miles beyond the ridge at Waterloo and 7 miles north-west of Ligny. Wellington rode out of Brussels at 7 am and overtook Picton's division, which had left at 4 am, on the road.

At Quatre Bras, where the great main road from Brussels to Charleroi is crossed almost at right-angles by one equally important from Nivelles to Namur, he found that there was no enemy in immediate view. A brigade of his Dutch troops had repulsed a probing attack by French cavalry the previous evening at the village of Frasnes, some miles further down the main road, and were now retreating.

Wellington at once ordered the Dutch troops to stand fast around the crossroads. Then, realising that Picton's division could not arrive before 11 am, he cantered off to the south-east to meet Blücher at Ligny, about to be attacked in strength. They arranged

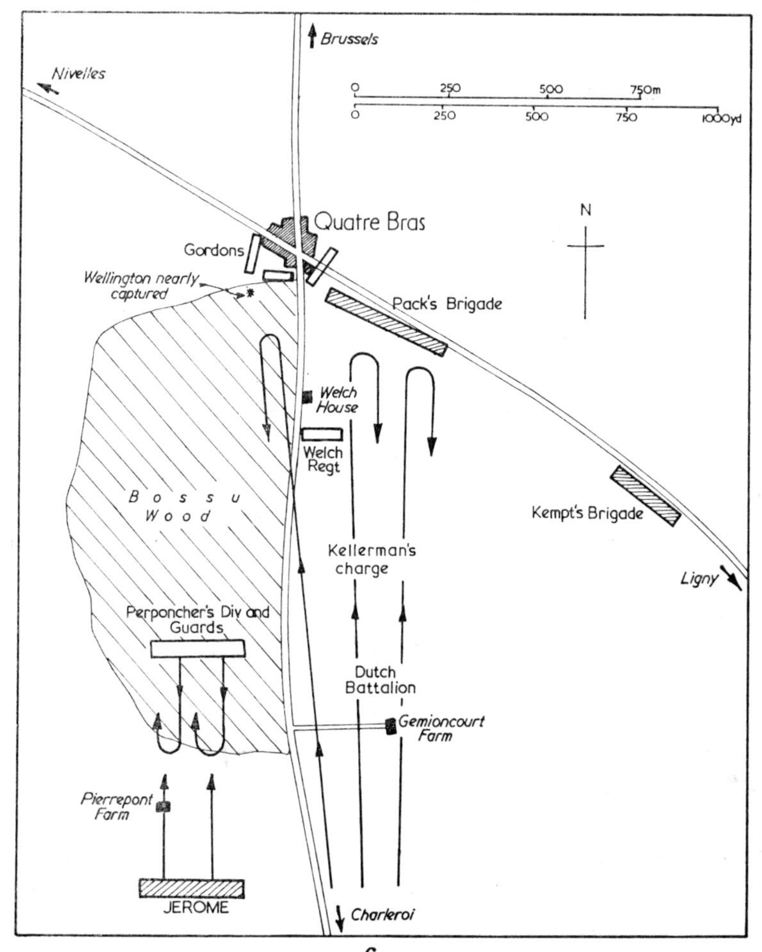

that if either man were driven back, he would converge on the probable line of withdrawal of the other. To prevent Napoleon from coming between them was only to observe the principles of concentration and cooperation in the face of the enemy.

Wellington then rode back to Quatre Bras, and realised the immense importance of the Nivelles–Namur road. It must be kept open as the great link between the two Allied armies.

The position of Quatre Bras is not unlike Waterloo in that it is at the top of a gradual easy rise whose crest gives a good position for infantry. Down the centre runs the great main road, Brussels to Charleroi, exactly bisecting the battlefield. From the crossroads and veering away to the south-west was a large wood, the wood of Bossu, 1½ miles long and 500 yards wide. On the other side of the main road and in front of the forward ridge stood the large farm-house of Gemioncourt.

A forced march brought Picton's division to the crossroads by 11 am, where Pack's leading brigade of the Royal Scots, Black Watch, Essex Regiment and the Gordon Highlanders took over an outpost position of Dutch-Belgian cavalry, and lined the Namur road running south-east from Quatre Bras. Kempt's brigade of the Gloucesters, Dukes and Camerons, arriving soon after, was sent to extend the left further and to deny that flank to the enemy. The Rifle Brigade went out to the far left of the line.

About 1 pm Ney advanced until held up by a Dutch battalion holding the farm of Gemioncourt. A protracted defence by the battalion delayed Ney's corps for a long time, and gained time for the steady arrival of other British and Allied units at the cross-roads. Perponcher's Dutch-Belgian division, moving round to the right, entered the wood of Bossu.

This wood, running parallel to the main road, was the most important tactical feature on the battlefield, and the obvious French line of advance. Wellington, feeling not fully confident that Perponcher's Dutch-Belgians were sufficient to hold the dangerous wood, sent two brigades of Guards on their arrival down to its forward edge.

At 3 pm Ney sent Jerome's division of 8,000 men and eight guns against Bossu Wood. The Dutch-Belgians were forced back into the wood just as the Guards arrived, and, the French attack was slowed down and finally held. About the same time a separate attack by the French in the centre had some success. Another uncoordinated French attack on Picton's division lining the road to Namur from Quatre Bras was driven back, though its left contingent nearly reached the crossroads, where the Gordons repulsed it.

During all these operations fresh regiments were arriving, and by 5 pm Wellington had a numerical superiority over the French, with 36,000 men against Ney's 22,000 – an unusual situation for any British army to find itself in when on the defensive.

On the repulse of the attack on Picton's division, Ney ordered Kellerman's cavalry brigade of 800 Cuirassiers to charge up the Brussels road, a hopeless task for so small a force against a well-disciplined deployed line. British regiments formed square, causing great casualties, but the impetus of the charging cavalry carried them up to the Namur road, on the way bursting through the ranks of the newly arrived Welch Regiment and seizing the King's Colour. (In 1909 Captain Jeffcock of the Inniskilling Dragoons, when on holiday in the Château country, saw this colour for sale in an antique shop at Azay-le-Rideau and bought it. It was the only colour ever lost in an army commanded by Wellington. Now very fragile, heavily netted and framed between glass, it is once again in the possession of the Welch Regiment, at Cardiff.)

The regiment has a story that the CO tried to conceal the loss of the colour, and that night set the regimental tailors to work to make a substitute that might pass as the original. However, this seems hardly possible. The tailors could scarcely have got at their gear in the first line transport that night, and it is extremely unlikely that any materials even remotely suitable would have been available. The next day a 10-mile march in pouring rain back to the ridge at Mont St Jean would not have left much time, opportunity, or inclination to get down again to fine sewing when greater affairs were afoot.

Wellington, anxious to show himself to the battalions that were undergoing a considerable ordeal, remained outside the squares. At one moment he found himself almost surrounded by individual French cavalrymen. Galloping up to the Gordon Highlanders, who were lining both sides of the main road at the crossroads, he shouted to them to lower their bayonets and to crouch low. This they did, and he then jumped the line, clearing the Highlanders easily and taking shelter in the square then forming.

It was claimed by some ill-informed people in London that Wellington's personal courage when under fire in the Peninsula had not been conspicuous. It seems possible that in the face of the French cavalry onslaught he deliberately staged this almost foolhardy act to prove the contrary.

At 7 o'clock the two Guards brigades were able to advance again in Bossu Wood, which they cleared, and soon afterwards two British brigades from the main position along the Namur road advanced astride the Brussels road. After 8 o'clock the Grenadiers moved out of Bossu Wood to Pierrepont Farm, several hundred yards in front. Ney's forces withdrew in the failing light from their forward positions, while the victors slept on the battlefield, some of the regiments having been on their feet for twenty hours.

Quatre Bras could so easily have been a victory for Ney. The British and their allies could have been pushed back, and Napoleon driven a wedge between them and the Prussians. Brussels could have been captured, Louis XVIII forced to leave the continent, and Napoleon have seated himself firmly in the saddle again. But Ney, a brave soldier but a mediocre general, and Napoleon between them made an appalling muddle over the employment of D'Erlon's corps.

At about 4 pm, under Ney's command, this corps of four divisions was moving north from Gosseilles through Frasnes towards Quatre Bras, as part of the main body. Without Ney being informed, it received orders direct from Napoleon to leave Ney and march at once back to Ligny, there to encircle Blücher's right flank. It was some time before Ney discovered that D'Erlon's corps had left him and, not knowing that it had been ordered back by Napoleon personally, he was understandably furious. Seeing that the chance of capturing the Quatre Bras crossroads was fading, Ney sent abrupt orders to D'Erlon to return at once. D'Erlon turned yet again, although he had now reached the edge of the Ligny battlefield, and marched back to Ney. Moving across country, the corps could not concentrate at Frasnes until 9 pm, by which time the action of Quatre Bras was over and darkness falling.

The corps fired not a shot all day, which was spent solely in waiting, marching and countermarching. Had Napoleon not recalled it from the Quatre Bras action, Wellington would have been overpowered. Had Ney not recalled it from Ligny, the

Prussian right flank would have been encircled and Blücher destroyed.

Two of the three buildings standing today at the great cross-roads of Quatre Bras are very old. They were there in 1815, and still show slight scars of battle. Unfortunately most Belgian farmers have a habit of lavishly plastering the upper walls of their farm-houses and barns with whitewash, thus covering up the bullet holes, though there is no doubt that they are still there. The farm buildings at the crossroads, which are unusually tall, must have received many hits. The tallest of the group, around which the Gordons fought, was standing in the mid-1960s, but has since been demolished to make way for a roadhouse for 'Le Dancing'. The positions of the squares, especially that of the Welch Regiment around which Kellerman's absurd cavalry charge roamed, are very clear and obvious.

When the French cavalry withdrew, Picton's two British brigades fell back slightly to avoid enemy artillery fire, and then resumed line formation. They were now only just in front of the vital Namur road. The retreat of the French cavalry had allowed the enemy guns to open up again, and the regiments, now once again very vulnerable, had little cover, though the narrow ditch on the north side of the road sheltered the Gloucesters and the Dukes for some time. This ditch can still be seen along the side of the road.

The wood of Bossu has entirely disappeared, the ground it covered now being under the plough. From the road to Nivelles, just to the west of the crossroads, one may obtain an excellent view of all the ground on which it stood. The wood formed a nasty obstacle on Wellington's right front, and tactically he was compelled to occupy it. If Ney had pushed hard and captured its southern edge, the defending Guards would have been badly embroiled in wood fighting. If Ney had exploited this in strength, he could have cleared the wood and found himself on the Nivelles road, behind the right flank of Picton's division holding the Namur road.

Marlborough was unhorsed at Ramillies and very nearly captured in a cavalry mêlée. Wellington too was caught up in the French cavalry charge on the Gordons at the crossroads, and he too could have been killed or captured. What might have been the results of such a disaster?

It would probably have had little effect immediately. The fresh regiments – there were not many more to come up around 5 pm when Wellington might have been killed or captured – were mainly filling gaps or reinforcing weak spots. The Battle of Quatre Bras was in fact fighting itself by the evening, and Wellington's personal presence and influence were barely necessary. Those regiments in the immediate vicinity would have been greatly shocked by Wellington's loss, but Pack's brigade would never have wavered. Bad news travels fast, but it must inevitably have taken a long time before such news reached the majority of the army. Meanwhile the British were getting stronger every hour and the French less active. The domination of Wellington's presence and personality was not an essential ingredient in the last few hours before darkness fell.

But the day after Quatre Bras would have shown the vast gap left by Wellington's disappearance. No general was ever more needed than he was in the ensuing forty-eight hours. The decision to withdraw about midday on the 17th, the choice of the area to be occupied, the implementation of the agreement with Blücher, the personal control during the withdrawal and, most important of all, the conduct of the great Battle of Waterloo, would have been unthinkable without Wellington.

He is credited with many sayings, and none was more apt than the one he spoke on the night after Waterloo: 'By God I don't think it would have done if I had not been there.' It is claimed that no man is indispensable. Wellington at Waterloo is the exception that proves the rule.

9 Waterloo: 1815

SITE *Twelve miles south of Brussels on the Charleroi–Reims road (N6 in Belgium, N5 in France).*
CONTESTANTS *The French army, under Napoleon, of 83,000 men, of whom 21,000 were cavalrymen, 10,000 artillerymen and 13,000 Imperial Guardsmen, with 350 guns. The Allies under Wellington, 105,000 men, of whom 14,000 were cavalrymen, and 8,000 artillerymen, with 200 guns. Of the Allies 34,000 were British, and 8,000 belonged to the King's German Legion. One Corps of 27,000 Prussian soldiers reached the battlefield just before the end.*
CASUALTIES *The French lost 30,000 killed and wounded, and all their guns. Their greatest losses were the shattering of their belief in Napoleon and in themselves as soldiers. The British lost 380 officers and 6,000 men, about 2,500 of whom were killed or died of wounds. The King's German Legion lost almost 25 per cent of its strength, while the Prussians lost 6,000 killed, wounded or missing.*

TODAY *There is much to be seen, with very little new building on the whole site. The visitor should not take any notice of the great mound, 100 feet high and surmounted by the British Lion, erected by the people of Brussels in the middle of the battlefield as an appreciation. It can be climbed, though, and of course offers a magnificent and all-embracing view. It is sited where Wellington said 'Stand up, Guards'. Many hours of absorbing interest can be spent at Waterloo.*

PRESENT ACCOMMODATION *Hotels in Brussels are plentiful. For real atmosphere the visitor might like to sleep at one of the two reasonable hotels in Waterloo itself. Both are quite adequate for one night.*

The three days from 16 to 18 June 1815 were some of the most momentous in world history. On the 16th Napoleon defeated the Prussian army at Ligny, while, only 5 miles away, Marshal Ney was being repulsed by the British under Wellington at Quatre Bras. Forty-eight hours later that same British army, supported at the end of the day by the Prussians, brought down Napoleon forever at Waterloo.

This most famous engagement was indeed one of the decisive battles of history. It saw the end of the Napoleonic legend and glamour. It saw the end of twenty-three years of French military adventure under perhaps the greatest Captain in history. It was the last of the many engagements between Great Britain and France – from 1066 to 1815 these almost hereditary enemies had fought thirty-two pitched battles. Apart from a year or two of occupation duties in Paris immediately after the battle, the British army left the continent for ninety-nine years, until Mons in 1914.

At dusk on the 16th and after the French under Ney had withdrawn from Quatre Bras, the British slept on the ridge they had held. On the 17th they withdrew northward for 9 miles to occupy a ridge already noted by Wellington as being tactically suitable for defence. As they marched, a torrential thunderstorm struck them, and on arrival at their respective posts, late in the evening with the rain still falling, they had to sleep out again with no shelter and little food. But they were about to make history.

The ridge of Mont St Jean, to give it its proper name, is little more than a slight rise. It is 3 miles long, facing south, and exactly bisected by the great main road, Charleroi to Brussels, today the N5. Along the crest of the ridge and at right-angles to the main road runs a lesser road from Nivelles to Wavre. The crossroads where they meet is the centre of the battlefield. About 300 yards south of the crossroads stood an imposing high-walled homestead, La Haye Sainte. Far off to the west and in front of the extreme right flank of the Allied army stands an even more imposing building, Le Château d'Hougoumont.

The light companies of four Guards battalions were sent down to hold the Château, while regiments of the line, interspersed with various allied contingents of Belgians, Hanoverians and Dutch were posted along the ridge. The remainder of the Guards

Brigade were placed slightly behind the main ridge and to the left rear of Hougoumont, lying down. On the north-east angle of the crossroads stood Lambert's Brigade of the King's Own, Inneskilling Fusiliers, the South Lancs and the Rifle Brigade. These regiments had landed from America at Ostend on 12 June and had marched to Ghent. On the evening of the 16th the brigade was called forward to Waterloo, and by a forced march of 48 miles in thirty hours reached the battlefield. As they marched through the village of Waterloo, 3 miles short of the ridge, they passed Wellington's billet. He came out on the balcony and acknowledged their cheers as they passed. To the left of Lambert's Brigade and lining the hedge along the road to Wavre stood the Gloucesters, Camerons and Royal Scots.

Immediately in front of the King's Own at the crossroads, and across the road to Wavre, lay a large gravel pit 50 yards wide and 200 yards long, running down the Charleroi road. This pit may still be seen. At their furthest advance the French infantry reached the northern edge of the gravel pit, being finally stopped by the fire of the King's Own behind their hedge only 20 yards away.

About 8 am the French army was ready to attack. It was lined up along a ridge almost parallel to the Allies, about half a mile away and in full view. Napoleon believed that the eighteen hours of heavy rain had so soaked the ground that horses could barely move out of a walk, and he decided to postpone offensive action for two or three hours. About 10 am he rode along his line reviewing the troops on his famous grey, in full view of the whole Allied line. The British junior officers and the men were fascinated to see at last and at such close quarters the most famous man in the World.

At 11.30 am the battle began with an attack on Hougoumont by the corps of Prince Jerome, Napoleon's younger brother (he lived until the age of seventy-five, dying in 1860). This attack was partially successful, lapping round the considerable grounds and orchard of the château. Some French soldiers reached the northern front of the main building, and one young French officer of great strength burst open the gate with an axe. He and a few men rushed in but were quickly killed. The gate was closed and Hougoumont remained in Allied hands for the remainder of the battle. Its capture, however, was still considered vital to Napoleon's plan, and the whole of the left corps, Reille's, was employed all day trying to reduce it.

Napoleon now decided to advance his infantry in strength northward astride the Charleroi road and, to soften up Wellington's line, ordered an enormous battery of eighty-four guns to form up. The battery, which included forty-four 12-pounders, took post on a low ridge about 250 yards south of La Haye Sainte and proceeded to deluge the defending infantry with fire. The British guns returned the fire, the noise being deafening. It was at this moment that Wellington, riding along his line, said: 'Hard pounding, Gentlemen. Let us see who can stand it the better.'

About 2 pm, and just as D'Erlon, the corps commander, was ready to lead the great mass of French regiments up the slight ridge to attack the outpost of La Haye Sainte and the gravel pit behind it, a great mass of moving troops was seen far out on the French right flank. A captured Prussian officer was brought to Napoleon, confirming the fear that it was the Prussian army marching under Blücher to Wellington's aid. The Emperor now realised that time, and the odds, were against him. At once he ordered D'Erlon to lead the 1st Corps of four divisions and four cavalry regiments, totalling 19,000 men, against the centre of the Allied line.

The left division assaulted La Haye Sainte, entirely surrounding it, and being met by close and efficient musketry fire from the men of the King's German Legion. The unit defending the homestead consisted of 337 excellent Hanoverian soldiers, recruited into and forming part of the British army. (Hanover was then one of the possessions of the British Crown, to remain so until the accession of Queen Victoria in 1837. It then became separated from Great Britain, as a woman could not be its ruler under the Salic Law.) The French infantry occupied the orchard and gardens but were unable to capture the farmhouse and barn.

On the right of the main road the French forced the Rifle Brigade out of the gravel pit by the crossroads, but being still in their mass formation, made an excellent target for the British regiments holding the hedges along the road. They were halted, having been very roughly handled, and were clearly wavering when two British cavalry brigades charged between the lines along the ridge and met French cavalry behind D'Erlon's now halted

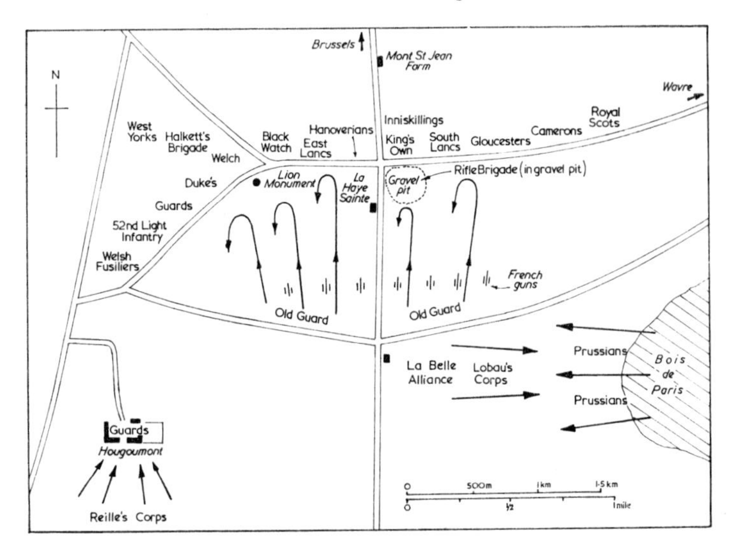

line. An inconclusive mêlée took place until the British cavalry withdrew, and soon after that D'Erlon's corps also retired, unimpeded by pursuit. Wellington had given the strictest orders that no infantry advance from the ridge to exploit a local success was to be made without his orders, and the French attempt to lure part of the British out of the main line failed.

Napoleon's next move was to launch 5,000 cavalrymen against Wellington's right centre, between Hougoumont and La Haye Sainte; they had to keep well clear of these two outposts to avoid the enfilade fire from their defenders. The Allies formed square, which was the usual counter to a cavalry attack, and the gunners were ordered to seek refuge within the squares when the enemy horsemen came close.

The attack, which started at 4 pm, was met by a hurricane of fire from the guns, whose teams were still manning them. The heavy uphill ground prevented the horses from moving faster than a trot, but the cavalry pressed on and, driving the gunners into the squares, penetrated what had been the line and rode between and behind the squares, suffering fearful casualties from the three rows of British infantrymen in each square firing at short range. Each square was, in fact, a miniature fortress, and none were broken by the enemy. Eventually the French horsemen withdrew, and the gunners ran forward to their guns, firing into the backs of the retreating enemy. Four times the French cavalry, driven off the ridge, reformed in the low ground out in front and returned to the charge. Each time they were repulsed, but the British squares were becoming smaller as casualties mounted, and the men more and more tired.

By 5 pm the leading Prussian division had advanced out of the Bois de Paris, about 12 miles east of La Haye Sainte, and Napoleon had to detach Count Lobau's Corps, so far in reserve, to hold them.

While the persistent French cavalry charges were being made, and repulsed, one brigade of D'Erlon's corps succeeded in advancing again and finally capturing La Haye Sainte. Ammunition for this isolated outpost had run out, and the French infantry fire had prevented any replenishment. The main farmhouse had caught fire when the French advanced troops succeeded in forcing an entry. The defenders had been reduced to forty-two men only, but they escaped singly back to the main British line.

The situation was critical for both Wellington and Napoleon. Wellington's squares, now thinly held and almost exhausted, formed a line that was by 8 pm tenuous in the extreme. One more determined cavalry charge might break it. The French, by capturing La Haye Sainte, were now firmly ensconced in a building only 300 yards in front of his weak centre. Wellington had no reserve left. Could he hold on until the Prussian attack took the pressure off him? He could see them heavily engaged with Lobau's corps, gradually forcing them back. Every minute gained was an asset.

Napoleon's situation was equally critical. He could see the Allied line thinning but his cavalry attacks were being repulsed time and again. He felt acute pressure on his right from the advancing Prussians. One final throw to defeat the Allied line would enable him to turn and meet his new enemy. Every minute lost was a liability. The Old Guard was at hand.

This corps d'élite had a glamour rarely approached in any army in history. Formed after Napoleon's first campaign in Italy, when he, as a young general, was not yet First Consul, it had been through all his campaigns from his great days of conquest during the years 1805 to 1810 to the retreat from Moscow. It had always been his trump card. On his escape from Elba and on reaching Paris, the reforming of the Old Guard had received high priority.

Every effort had been made to trace the fit members of the Guard that had been disbanded on his first abdication, and they had been re-enlisted into the Old Guard, whose ranks had then been completed with specially selected NCOs and men from the line regiments. Experienced soldiers aged about thirty were ideal candidates. Many of the older soldiers had been in the revolutionary army at Valmy as boys in 1792, twenty-three years previously and had been in each of Napoleon's great battles. The Old Guard was, at Waterloo, as efficient and trustworthy as ever it had been. It had never failed, and it must now surely break the stubborn immovable British squares.

The Guard tramped up the slight slope to the ridge in mass formation, 13,000 of them. Marshal Ney, the Bravest of the Brave, had been put in direct personal command over the head of the existing Guards commander, Marshal Mortier, Napoleon's oldest friend. As the front line of battalions passed alongside La Haye Sainte, Ney's horse was shot from under him, but, declining the offer of his own horse by a junior officer behind him, he led the Guard on foot. On they came, the target of all the British guns still in action, suffering terrible casualties but apparently irresistable. Their centre was directly approaching the right of Halkett's brigade. Behind it were three battalions of Guards, lying down in a slight hollow and out of sight of the advancing Old Guard. Wellington, mounted, was behind the Guards.

Suddenly he called out 'Stand up, Guards. Load, Fire!' The much quoted 'Up Guards and at 'em' is without foundation. At once the French saw on their left front a wall of scarlet suddenly built; but they were in column, and so only sixty men in each front rank could fire at the same time. While a line formation was being taken up, Colin Halkett's brigade, with the Dukes and the Welch in front in line, moved slightly forward and opened fire at the French left flank. The Old Guard paused, feeling this opposition on its left, and one of its regiments, the 4th Grenadiers, moved out to assault the two British battalions. Both suffered severely from the close musketry fire, and from two 8-pounder guns the Old Guard had dragged forward by hand. In this little area a bloody stalemate was developing.

The 52nd Light Infantry, later the Oxford and Bucks LI, had also been lying down beyond the Guards and out of sight.

Wellington galloped up to the CO, who had already alerted his battalion and was wheeling it round to its left, and shouted to the Colonel 'Go on, Colborne, go on. They won't stand. Fire'. Colborne halted his battalion of 1,000 men in two lines, exactly covering the left flank of the Old Guard, and opened fire at its centre. The effect was devastating at this 40 yards' range. The converging fire of the Dukes, the Welch, the Foot Guards, and now the 52nd was too much. Owing to their massed formation, the Frenchmen could not deploy or form a line to meet the fire on their flank; only the few men on the outer flank could return fire as best they could.

Wellington, with marvellous perception, sensed a sudden drastic change in French morale in front of him. There were incredulous cries of 'La Garde recule'. It was just after 8 pm. Suddenly, after a cloudy and overcast day, the sun came out and Wellington was seen by nearly his whole army. Seizing his chance, he stood in his saddle, removed his cocked hat, and, waving it above his head, pointed it at the enemy. The Allied army almost to a man moved forward. The Old Guard broke and melted into a stream of fugitives in full flight all along the line. The Battle of Waterloo was over.

Much disorder arose in the low ground out beyond the Ridge. The exultant British soldiers, suddenly released from enemy fire and able to move again, forgot all fatigue and swarmed on. A few French regiments stood and resisted for a while, but they were soon isolated, in the sea of, admittedly, a virtually disorganised Allied army.

The Prussians, although tired after almost two days' marching, were psychologically and nervously fresh and they carried on the pursuit. The beating of their drums and blowing of bugles created panic in the fleeing French ranks, and as darkness fell, complete chaos ensued.

Wellington rode slowly forward and at La Belle Alliance, a large inn on the main road half a mile beyond La Haye Sainte, he met Marshal Blücher. Cooperation had triumphed.

By virtue of its proximitiy to the great city of Brussels, only 12 miles away, and its position across the great highway to Charleroi, Reims, Dijon and the south, Waterloo is much visited. It is perhaps the most popular battlefield in the world for the travelling historian and the ordinary visitor. It far exceeds Hastings in interest, although the latter had an even greater impact on history.

There is much to be seen on the battlefield – the ridge, Hougoumont, La Haye Sainte, the gravel pit, the hedge along the Wavre road, La Belle Alliance are all still there. The walls of the orchard at Hougoumont still show signs of the loopholing made by the Guards, while around the south gateway and its great door can be seen bullet marks.

La Haye Sainte has not been rebuilt, and the walls enclosing the farmyard are untouched. The farmhouse has a new roof. The gravel pit, no longer in use, is now filled with undergrowth. Wellington's billet in Waterloo village is now a little museum and well worth a visit.

The most interesting building of all played no part in the battle. Le Ferme du Caillou, 6 miles south of the battlefield on the main road, is a square and dignified eighteenth-century manor house, with garden and drive at the back and an imposing gateway. Here Napoleon slept the night before the battle. On the ground floor are his dining-room and bedroom, all untouched since 1815. In the dining-room stands the table where he dined, with its original tablecloth. A silver plate from which he breakfasted on the morning of Waterloo is in the possession of the Duke of Richmond and on view at Goodwood House. It was the present Duke's great-great-great-grandmother who gave the famous ball in Brussels the night before Quatre Bras.

Showcases have been provided at Le Ferme du Caillou, all containing relics of uniforms, arms, medals, domestic items, saddlery etc. Napoleon's great travelling coach was parked on the drive behind the house. The main gate, which was built a few years after the battle, has vertical ribs fashioned like French bayonets.

In the field to the north of the house Napoleon's personal bodyguard of one battalion bivouacked in the rain all night. Some of his senior officers slept upstairs (now the quarters of the caretaker, and not open to visitors), and the horses of the more important officers were sheltered in a few stables at the back. Few people seem to know of this romantic little house, and, whereas the field of Waterloo always has many visitors, especially on Sunday afternoons, few people came to Le Ferme du Caillou.

10 Gravelotte: 1870

SITE *Five miles west of Metz on the Metz–Verdun–Paris main road, N3.*

CONTESTANTS *The French regular army, nominally under Napoleon III but in fact under Marshal Bazaine. The Prussian army under Von Moltke.*

NUMBERS *The French had 80,000 men, with 450 guns, and the Prussians 120,000, with 730 guns.*

CASUALTIES *The French lost 13,000 men, 90 per cent of whom were taken prisoner when Metz surrendered at the end of the war. The Prussians lost 5,000 killed, 14,000 wounded, with 500 missing.*

PRESENT ACCOMMODATION *Excellent hotels in Metz, 5 miles off, and Verdun, 30 miles away. Gravelotte, being on the great main road, N3, is extremely easy to find. The little museum in the centre of the village is of great interest. Motoring roads are, of course, excellent.*

The causes of the Franco-Prussian War, to end so disastrously for France, were complex. The French, led by the Emperor with the magic name Napoleon, regarded the military development of Prussia with concern, and Napoleon III believed, with some justification, that war should be sought before Prussia became very much stronger. France was quite ready for an excuse, although not really good enough to engage a major European power.

In July 1870 the throne of Spain was suddenly offered to Prince Leopold of Hohenzollern-Sigmaringen, a member of the Prussian Royal House. France felt, understandably, that to have a warlike and growing Prussia to the east and, across the Pyrenees, the Spaniards under a Prussian monarch was too much. She therefore made strong protests to Berlin, and the crisis passed when Prince Leopold withdrew his acceptance of Spain's throne. France then demanded that not only would King William I publicly associate himself with the abandonment of the candidature, but also give a guarantee that it would not be revived. This insane proposal [illegible] utt[illegible] by t[illegible] K[illegible]g, who refused to see the French [illegible]e declared war on Prussia.

[illegible] start. Firstly, the Prussian army [illegible]ur to three, and her mobilisation [illegible]uicker and efficient. She had the [illegible]dvantage she retained until 1945, [illegible] three great men – Bismarck, the [illegible]nan Europe had ever seen; Von [illegible]t Headquarters; and Von Moltke, [illegible]able as the others.

[illegible]f her Emperor, whose uncle had [illegible] and who was remembered by all [illegible]d the new Chassepot rifle, which [illegible] rifle, she was eager to avenge the imagined insult of her envoy.

Napoleon III was officially the generalissimo, but his lack of military knowledge quickly showed itself and he handed over to Marshal Bazaine the command of the southern half of the French army fourteen days after the outbreak of war. That army moved eastwards towards Strasbourg and then across the German frontier, the southern half under Bazaine being quickly defeated at Weissemburg, whence it withdrew in considerable confusion through Metz, using only two of the several bridges available. The individual corps moved on to the high ground to the west of the town and lined the main Verdun–Metz road, the N3. The Prussians followed, crossing the Moselle further upstream, and then, wheeling right, came up to the line of villages along the main road.

On 16 and 17 August these villages – Mars-la-Tour, Rezonville, and Vionville – were captured by the Prussians, who evicted the respective French corps occupying them with difficulty. The French withdrew into the night and Von Moltke, the Prussian Commander-in-Chief (uncle of the Von Moltke who was such a dismal failure as German C-in-C in August 1914), did not know for many hours where they had gone. It seems surprising that strong cavalry patrols were not sent out to scout for the French. The ground is most suitably for cavalry, for the woods are small and infrequent, long easy ridges give superb viewpoints, and the going is good.

Bazaine had in fact withdrawn his severely defeated troops north-eastwards and taken up a defensive position facing west along the high ground just east of Gravelotte. Oddly enough, the two armies were now precisely at right-angles to each other. The French left near Ars-sur-Moselle and the Prussian right near Rezonville were barely 3 miles apart, whereas their outer flanks were separated by 14 miles.

The position taken up by Bazaine was not tactically bad. It lay largely along a broad ridge facing west about 5 mile west of Metz and just east of the crossroads of Gravelotte. His left flank was protected by the thick Bois de Vaux, standing on a steep hillside. An advance up this incline through woods would render any attacker quite breathless and incapable of active movement on reaching the open high ground at the top. In the centre the partly entrenched line ran along the western edge of the ridge in front of Moscou Farm, Leipsic Farm, St Hubert Farm and Le Point du Jour. This part of the line also overlooked a wooded ravine, although less steep and less severe than the one on the left. Further north it was extended rather weakly and dangerously up to the crossroads at the hamlet of St Privat. Altogether the front stretched over 7 miles.

Bazaine, always a timid general, was obsessed by the importance of Metz, not only because of its position in the permanent French eastward-facing line of defence but also because of the shelter it could offer to the army if unduly pressed. Accordingly he placed his reserves behind his strong left flank, already in a virtually impregnable position. They were not utilised at all during the battle and merely joined their comrades in Metz at the end of the battle to become prisoners of war. Had they been posted behind the right of the line, they might well have turned the scales against the Prussians.

The first move was by the Prussians, who, still not certain where their enemy was, advanced over the N3 and then, wheeling right, carried out a gigantic change of direction to come face to face

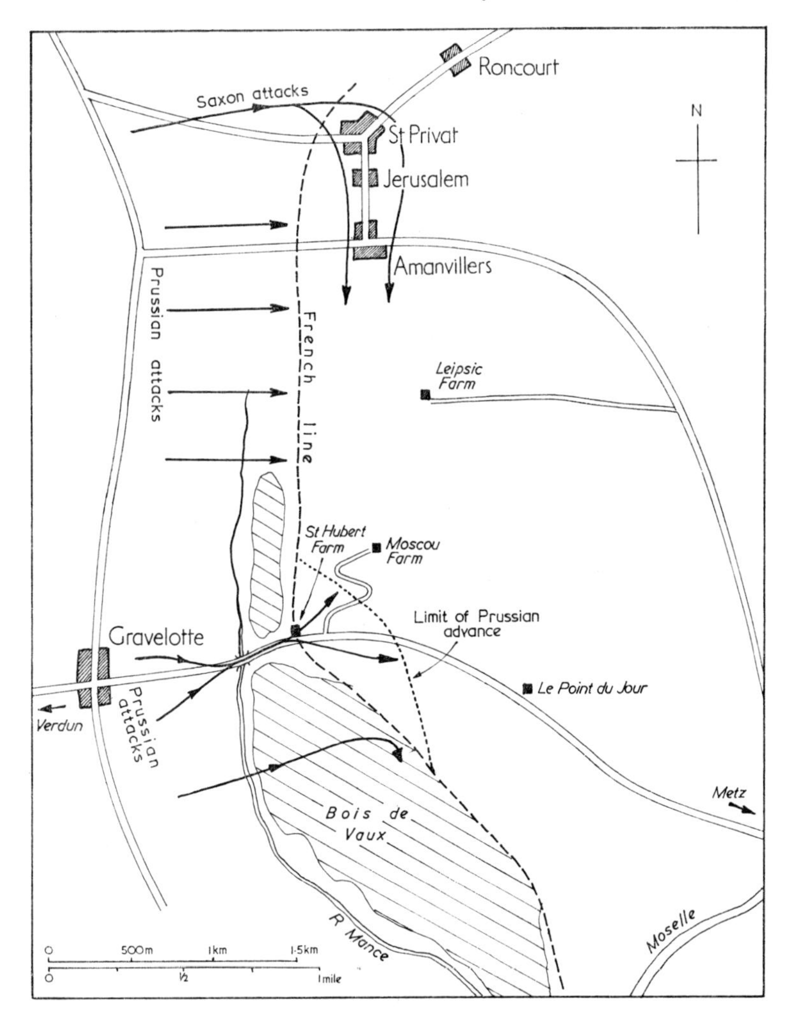

with the French army along its newly entrenched position on the high ground.

The Battle of Gravelotte had three areas of conflict. On the Prussian right an army corps attacked the strong French left, and was bloodily repulsed. The best French troops were holding the high ground above the Bois de Vaux, whereas the attacking Prussians not only had the steep hillside to climb but in addition had great difficulty in keeping direction in the woods covering the incline. The Farms of Point du Jour, St Hubert, and Moscou were heavily bombarded and set on fire, but the left of the French line held. Another corps was sent in astride the main Gravelotte–Metz road.

The new attack had to descend the defile leading to the only bridge over the little stream, the Mance. This bridge, the only one for many miles over the wide swampy river bed of the Mance, inevitably caused a bottleneck, covered by French artillery fire from St Hubert's Farm. The advancing Prussian infantry had to deploy, cross the little stream on a wide front, avoiding the bridge, and then toil up the opposite slope. On emerging into the open they were met by close-range French musketry but managed to surround St Hubert's Farm, which they captured.

A fearsome crush had now developed at the bridge over the Mance; cavalry and the engineers with their equipment all had to use the bridge, the little valley being impassable except for infantry. The French artillery, although denied St Hubert's as an observation post, got the range accurately. The left wing of the French, still holding on the high ground above the Bois de Vaux, provided a good view of the bridge, the artillery fire was directed therefrom, and great chaos ensued in the defile.

After the fall of St Hubert's Farm, the Prussians tried to advance north-east to Moscou Farm, on the highest point of the plateau, but failed owing to the musketry of the French infantry using their new Chassepot rifle. Leipsic and Point du Jour Farms also held out, so that, apart from the success at St Hubert's Farm, the Prussians had achieved little. As darkness fell, there was much skirmishing among small units and the confusion became overwhelming. But fatigue eventually intervened, the fighting died down, and soon after 10 pm the order was given to cease fire. Stalemate had occurred but Bazaine's reserve was still unused.

Out on the French right a strong Prussian attack against the villages of Roncourt and St Privat had been held, again owing to the excellence of French musketry. The casualties inflicted on the attackers were very high, 50 per cent of the officers and 30 per cent of the men being hit, and it seemed to Bazaine that, with his left flank secure, his centre barely dented and his right holding, he was winning the battle. But now the absence of a reserve on his right was to be felt acutely.

A final last desperate attack by a Saxon brigade supported by brilliant artillery fire succeeded in capturing St Privat. Turning right it started to roll up the French line from the north, meeting with great success, largely owing to the brittle morale of the French soldiers. A counterattack by a reserve immediately available would have stopped the already somewhat disorganised Saxon brigade, have bolstered French morale, restored the whole of the right flank, and caused Von Moltke to think hard. He, by now, had no reserve left.

But it was not to be. The collapse of the French right wing extended southward for a mile, taking in its stride the little hamlet of Jerusalem. The exultant Saxons pressed on beyond Amanvillers but there darkness halted them too and the whole of the northern part of the battlefield became quiet. Both armies slept on the ground for the night.

Next morning at dawn the Prussian left wing moved forward cautiously, to push back the already deflated French army. But they need not have bothered. The French had left the battlefield before dawn and streamed eastward off the plateau into the welcoming shelter of Metz. This move, decided upon by Bazaine, had already been anticipated by his corps and divisional commanders. Even the undefeated French around St Hubert and Moscou Farms, and the uncommitted reserve on the ground above the Bois de Vaux gave up their lines and retired.

The Prussians left four army corps to besiege Metz, but they and the French in the fortress took no further part in the campaign. The remainder of Von Moltke's victorious army marched off to the west towards Châlons-sur-Marne to join the Prussian force about to win the Battle of Sedan.

Bazaine as a soldier was a sorry figure. Born in 1811, the year before the retreat from Moscow and four years before Waterloo, he had served for forty years in the French Regular Army. He enlisted as a private soldier in 1831, became a sergeant within a year and then transferred to the Foreign Legion. He saw active service in Algeria and in Spain, and in 1833 was commissioned as sous-lieutenant. By 1854 he was commanding his regiment, and then a brigade, in the Crimea. In 1859 he became a general and was in action at Solferino; and in 1862 he took his division on the Mexican campaign, to the chief command of which he succeeded in 1863. He was promoted Marshal of France in 1864, and married in 1865, when he was fifty-four.

By 1870, when he was fifty-nine, he was clearly the most experienced senior officer in the French army, but he had become very stout, and was well past his prime. As Commander-in-Chief he was defeated in the field by his country's invaders, besieged in one of his country's most famous fortresses, and forced to surrender. At the end of hostilities he was court-martialled and imprisoned. Surely no general has ever tasted such a bitter cup of defeat.

It is best to approach Gravelotte from the west, along the Verdun–Metz road, thereby passing through the villages of Mars-la-Tour, Vionville, and Rezonville. At the crossroads of Gravelotte the museum and the house where Napoleon III slept the night before the battle should be visited. Still moving east, and now downhill, you may cross the valley of the Mance on an imposing embankment, whence the Bois de Vaux is very evident, with the stream far below the road emerging from a little culvert.

Move up the hill to St Hubert's Farm and the French front line, thence left-handed along a poor farm track to Moscou Farm, today a modern sugar refinery. In a cottage garden alongside the track is a French gun carriage deep in grass. The barrel has gone and the metal fittings are rusting away, but it makes a most interesting 'find'. The view all around is superb, and the ground most suitable for cavalry or, today, tanks.

Return to Gravelotte, there turning right along the N390 and then the D11 for St Privat. Turn right and so drive down the right flank of the French front line, which, if it had held, could have caused a Prussian defeat.

11 Sedan: 1870

SITE *Sedan is 150 miles north-east of Paris on the N64, 8 miles from the Luxemburg frontier at Bouillon.*

CONTESTANTS *The Third Prussian Army, under the Crown Prince Frederick (Von Moltke supervising), with 200,000 men and 770 guns. The French 'Army of Châlons' under Marshal Macmahon (badly wounded in the battle, and replaced by de Wimpfen), with 120,000 men and 560 guns. The Emperor Napoleon III was present throughout the action but took no part tactically or in command.*

CASUALTIES *The Prussians lost 2,300 killed, with 6,000 wounded. The French had 17,000 killed and wounded, and 21,000 were taken prisoner.*

NOTE *The Franco-Prussian War was the first in which railways played a part. They were much used in bringing divisions up to the front, after mobilisation, and for providing a steady stream of food, ammunition and supplies. The wounded were evacuated by hospital trains.*

PRESENT ACCOMMODATION *The Hôtel de l'Europe in the Place de la Gare in Sedan is Excellent, and Le Strasbourg is adequate. Excellent motoring, and taxi drivers at the station know their history.*

General Bazaine's conduct of his half of the French campaign ended with his defeat at Gravelotte on 18 August, and his withdrawal into the fortress of Metz. Neither he nor his army of 80,000 men took any further effective part in the Franco-Prussian War. A fortnight later the other half of the French army, under Macmahon, was beaten at Sedan, with the capture of the Emperor Napoleon III, who was removed to Germany as a prisoner of war.

Macmahon's defeat at Wörth on 6 August, the long march back to the west, and the defeat of one of his corps at Beaumont, where it was surprised in bivouac after dark with the loss of 7,000 men and forty-two guns, had greatly lowered the morale of his men. The French army staggered into Sedan during 31 August, not really caring anything about what might happen. The security of a fortress promised rest, food, and billets, all the soldiers wanted.

Sedan was far from suitable defensively. The unfordable Meuse ran south and just west of the town, crossed by bridges at Donchery to the west, and near Bazeilles, 3 miles south-east of Sedan. To the north lay a gradually rising triangle of land, in the the centre of which lay a large wood, the Bois de Garenne. Down the eastern side of the triangle towards Bazeilles ran a steep escarpment at the foot of which ran a stream through the villages of Givonne, Daigny and La Moncelle.

The Prussians had very good artillery and at their leisure they could bombard the town from east and west, and neutralise Bazeilles, without committing any infantry at the start of the battle at all.

One French corps occupied the north-west side of the triangle. The 1st Corps occupied the east-facing side of the triangle holding the escarpment, with considerable forces over the little River Givonne, with its artillery back on the higher ground behind. To the south one corps prolonged the right, and, extending southward, included Bazeilles. In the town the 5th Corps was in reserve.

The Commander of the Prussian Third Army on the west side of the Meuse was Frederick, the Crown Prince of Russia. His wife, the Crown Princess, later the Empress Frederick, was the eldest daughter of Queen Victoria. He succeeded his father, William I, the first German Emperor, eighteen years after Sedan, but only reigned for three months, tragically dying of cancer of the throat.

Crown Prince Frederick began the Battle of Sedan by pushing northward on the west side of the Meuse, towards the bridge over the river at Donchery, which the leading corps found to be intact. A detachment of French engineers had been sent out by train from Sedan to destroy this bridge, but when the men had detrained, the engine driver drove off at top speed with all the tools and explosives. A second party to arrive to do the job found the bridge occupied by the enemy. The Crown Prince pushed on and started to threaten the north-west face of the great triangle.

On arrival at Bazeilles the Bavarians found the bridge over the Meuse also undamaged, but could see the French soldiers preparing it for demolition. They rushed the bridge, threw the powder barrels into the river, and moved up to the outskirts of the village. But they were counterattacked and forced back to the river. Macmahon ordered the bridge to be blown up at once, but another muddle prevented this being done. By now the Bavarian field engineers had thrown two temporary pontoon bridges across the river, and with two of the three main bridges already in their hands, the Prussians could execute a gigantic pincer movement, always a favourite among German tacticians.

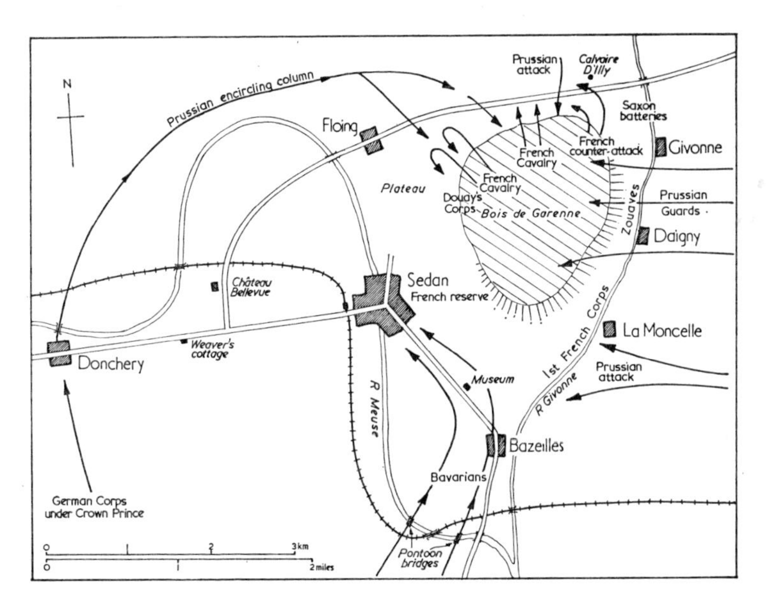

Out to the east the Saxons advanced on a wide frontage and halted just beyond the little Givonne stream. By this last move Sedan and the French army were practically surrounded, but Von Moltke was still not satisfied. Late at night on 31 August, accompanied by the King, he visited the Crown Prince's headquarters. Here he ordered the part of the corps that had crossed the

Donchery bridge to move further north and seal off all possible French escape routes to the west.

Before dawn on 1 September the Prussians crossed the Meuse by the old bridge and the new pontoons near Bazeilles. The French pickets on the river bank had withdrawn and the village, half a mile over the river, was reached without the alarm being given. Why the French had neglected to post guards at these bridges will never be known, for a prolonged resistance here must have held up the crossing for many hours. As it was, the enemy were able to capture Bazeilles and create a nasty threat to the right flank of the two eastward-facing French Corps. This thrust also opened a road into the heart of the Fortress, there being no French troops between Bazeilles and Sedan.

The French, although surprised in the village, defended it gallantly. Fires caused by German shells were now added to by both sides, who deliberately set alight many houses to smoke out their opponents. Many French civilians unwisely helped their troops, and all those captured by the attackers were immediately shot. The last ditch quality of many of the desperate little local engagements was the subject of the famous picture 'La Dernière Cartouche'.

About 6 am, as the light grew stronger, the fighting in Bazeilles died down. The commander of the 1st Corps could now see a vast German horde approaching the escarpment from the east. They halted to position their guns and then attacked the Givonne river line. Sixteen batteries covered the advance on the left, which captured the village of La Moncelle and then linked up with the Bavarians at Bazeilles.

The great Prussian advance spread up the Givonne valley and threatened the next village, Daigny, but there it was held up by Zouaves. It was nearly 10 am before this village fell. The French withdrew, losing several guns, and as they scrambled up their steep escarpment, the German guns severely harassed them, killing the French divisional commander.

About this time the French Commander-in-Chief, Macmahon, rode out from Sedan towards Bazeilles to assess the situation there. On his way a shell fragment hit him in the leg, completely incapacitating him, and he was carried back into the town, handing over to General de Wimpfen.

At 4 am the Crown Prince's leading units had began to cross the river at Donchery. By 8 am they had reached the Sedan–Mezières road and there marched eastward, finally to complete the circle round the doomed French army. The artillery of both German corps formed up on the high ground to the north of a big ravine, and the infantry, passing through the Prussian guns, advanced south-east to the attack. As they crossed the Floing–Illy road, they were charged by a strong force of French cavalry, but the charge was held by the rifle fire of the infantry and the guns, and the French cavalry broke. Soon they were scattered in confusion. Some men regained their own lines, but the majority, disorganised and in little parties, galloped away northward and rode off into the hills and woods of the Ardennes. Some of these men found their way round to Mezières, where they later formed part of a hotch-potch army collected in north-east France after Napoleon's surrender to harass the Prussian forces there during the advance to Paris. In this little sub-campaign several engagements took place around Bapaume and Péronne, and in the streets of villages well known in the Battle of the Somme in 1916.

The little gap made by the French cavalry did not remain open for long. The Guards coming up on the left of the Saxons attacked across the Givonne valley, while their cavalry swept round to the right and, shortly before midday, there joined hands with the 5th German Corps, so finally closing the circle.

By mid-morning the sun had come out and the King of Prussia, with Von Moltke and the headquarters staff, found a viewpoint on high ground. From it they could see the streets of Sedan, the smoke from the guns on the Floing heights, and Bazeilles burning in the distance, and they could hear the guns firing at the escarpment, and see shells bursting in the Bois de Garenne.

It was the last occasion on which a reigning monarch saw his army go into action. Beside the King stood his Commander-in-Chief, Von Moltke; his Secretary of War, Von Roon; Bismarck, the Iron Chancellor; and officials from the War Office and Foreign Office. Colonel Walker from the British army in his capacity as military attaché in Berlin, General Sheridan from the USA, Mr Russell of *The Times* and a dozen German minor princelings were there. The members of the last-mentioned group were seeing the independence of their little states dwindling by the hour.

About 11 am General Ducrot, feeling pressure on the left flank of his troops defending the escarpment, rode through the Bois de Garenne and found that the enemy had occupied a little hill, the Calvaire D'Illy, and could now fire down into the great wood behind his main position. He collected together what men he could find and flung them into a sort of counterattack against the Calvaire. But the German IX Corps had now massed ninety guns to the north-west and, temporarily abandoning their present target of the Bois, turned their fire on the tentative counterattack. It was too much for the French and they broke, in full retreat to the supposed shelter of the Bois de Garenne.

About the same time German infantry had pressed forward and emerged on to the plateau to the north-west running back to the Bois de Garenne. The situation here was critical in the extreme for the French, and called for extreme measures. General Margueritte was ordered to charge, with his cavalry brigade, the Prussian infantry division now establishing itself on the edge of the plateau. Although Margueritte was badly wounded in the mouth as the great charge started, it went forward with the customary élan of the French advance. Starting at a trot, the charge quickly increased to a gallop, and, the ground being slightly downhill, it soon became an irresistible avalanche that no troops could halt. The forward elements of the German advance were swept aside but then the three cavalry regiments came up against the steadfast German infantry with their new breech-loading rifles. Discipline again won, and the great charge broke as the cavalrymen were shot from their saddles. The few survivors from the centre joined up again with the right-hand party, and under their new commander, General Gallifet, made another attempt. They too failed. The Prussian King from his lookout was heard to murmur 'Les braves gens', words now carved on the French War Memorial at Floing. Legend says that as the last survivors passed along the front of a German regiment, the Germans ceased fire and the officers saluted.

Douay's Corps now began to disintegrate, as the infantry sought what shelter from the artillery fire they could in the Bois. The collapse, starting on the left, rolled along to the right, and soon there was no French line on the north-west of the great Sedan triangle.

Another break in the line came in the north-east, where the defenders also fled to the woods. Here the Saxons had managed to cross the Givonne stream not only with their infantry but also with their guns, and had established several lines of batteries. Each of the ten batteries now took on a different section of the wood, and each gun was fired with a different elevation. As a result few corners of the wood escaped the fire. It was a 'carpet-bombardment', a forerunner of the aerial 'carpet-bombing' of 1944 and 1945.

About 2.30 pm, all the guns ceased fire, and the Guards infantry advanced into the wood. Masses of demoralised French soldiers had piled arms and now waved white handkerchiefs in surrender. Their morale had collapsed, as had their organisation and structure of command. All that remained was to surrender. By 5 pm the corps under the Crown Prince joined hands with the Guards and the Saxons, and the wood and its thousands of occupants was in Prussian hands.

At Bazeilles the last post to hold out before the Prussians advanced to the southern edge of Sedan was the end cottage of a row of four running back from the main road between the two villages. It was held by a small detachment of French marines who, from the windows of the upper floor, had excellent targets down the road and in the little courtyard below. They fired until every cartridge was used, and then, surrendering, were allowed to march out into captivity.

Napoleon had spent the day riding round the battlefield, trying to find a hero's death in action. But he was unsuccessful, and, hearing of the collapse on the north-west side, hoisted the white flag in Sedan. Seeing the flag, Von Moltke sent an emissary to the city to enquire its full meaning. He brought back the famous message:

> Not having been able to die in the midst of my troops, there is nothing left for me but to surrender my sword into your Majesty's hands. I am your Majesty's faithful brother, Napoleon.

Until receipt of this letter neither King William nor Bismarck knew Napoleon was in Sedan. They studied it carefully and then replied, in the King's name, that an officer of high rank must come out to receive the terms of surrender. That evening General de Wimpfen, accompanied by one of Napoleon's personal staff, rode out to a weaver's cottage near Donchery where Bismarck and Von

Moltke awaited him. After several hours of argument, in which the Prussians held all the cards, de Wimpfen finally agreed to the unconditional surrender of the whole French army. He rode back into the town and told Napoleon that nothing less would satisfy Von Moltke. But the Emperor decided to approach the King himself, appealing as one monarch to another for understanding and cooperation within their own magic royal circle.

Early next morning he drove out to Donchery to find the King. Near the weaver's cottage he met Bismarck, who listened politely to Napoleon's case but declined to let him see the King until he had received Napoleon's word that complete surrender would be implemented. Meanwhile, de Wimpfen, seeing the inevitable, had gone to the Château Bellevue where, meeting Von Moltke, he signed the surrender terms. Bismarck, still talking with Napoleon at the weaver's cottage half a mile away, was at once informed and, sending for the King, took Napoleon to the Château. Here the two monarchs had a brief and embarrassing interview. In addition to congratulating King William on his victory, Napoleon spoke of his great admiration for the Prussian artillery, always Germany's most efficient weapon. He then asked that he might be driven away into captivity through Belgium, so that only a minimum of his French soldiers would see him and his humiliation.

Of all the towns in France whose name is associated with a great battle, none has more to show today than Sedan. The weaver's cottage with the same windows and doors, roof and drainpipes, is completely unchanged. The grass on which Napoleon and Bismarck had their chairs is still the same grass.

The Château Bellevue, where Napoleon and King William formally met, is quite easily found. It has been extended since 1870, but the main façade is quite unmistakable. The very clearly expressed 'Propriété Privée' notices precludes any visits.

The escarpment running north and south to the east of the Bois de Garenne is much higher and steeper than anticipated. It forms a superb defensive position for 2 miles, and everywhere overlooks the quite considerable Givonne stream, flowing along its base, which the Germans had to cross before assaulting the ridge. It says a great deal for the excellence of the attacking German infantry that they so successfully pushed the French up the escarpment and into the Bois de Garenne.

The Bois is still very thick with trees. The shells from the 'carpet-bombardment' detonating on its trees created havoc and utter demoralisation among the masses of French soldiers pushed back into the wood.

The house at Bazeilles where the last stand was made is now an excellent museum, with the famous picture 'La Dernière Cartouche' in the post of honour. Two rooms downstairs are filled with showcases containing innumerable relics. Upstairs are three rooms, two of which figured in the famous picture. Nothing is changed. The bullet holes in the great wardrobe in the picture are still visible, and there are many others in the walls facing the windows from which the French soldiers fired at their enemies in the yard below. The ceiling has its share of holes, and the outer walls of the house show the scars of many Prussian bullets.

One interesting relic is a tattered Union Jack from a British horse-drawn ambulance, one of four sent by the British Government to demonstrate its sympathy with Napoleon.

Near the present iron bridge over the Meuse to the south of Bazeilles, on the site of the one the French failed to blow up, are traces of two brief roadways cut into the steep and deep river banks. They are the last vestiges of the entry and exits of the pontoon bridges thrown over the Meuse by the Prussians.

12 Mons: 1914

SITE *The bank of the canal circling the north of the town and then running west towards Valenciennes. Mons is about 35 miles south-west of Brussels on the Paris road, N7.*

CONTESTANTS *The British 1st and 2nd Army Corps, consisting of the 1st, 2nd, 3rd and 5th Infantry Divisions and 19th Independant Infantry Brigade, all under Field-Marshal Sir John French. Total 80,0000 men, 328 guns. Four German army corps and two cavalry divisions, totalling 180,000 men, probably with 500 guns.*

CASUALTIES *The British army lost 1,600 killed, wounded or missing, almost half of them coming from the Royal Irish and the Middlesex regiments. Those of the Germans were far higher, owing to the superb musketry and machine-gun fire of the British infantry battalions, and the German habit of attacking in mass, moving as though on a parade ground. They did not adopt the 'extended order', or 'deployment formations' used by the British until the First Battle of Ypres, October 1914. Their total loss is unknown but may well have been 15,000.*

PRESENT ACCOMMODATION *Mons is not recommended. Good hotels at Tournai, 25 miles, and Brussels, 35 miles. Roads good but many mining villages, slagheaps, and railway lines immediately to the south of Mons.*

In World War I four place-names became almost household words to the British people – Mons, Ypres, the Somme and Gallipoli. Ypres stood for horror, the Somme for tragedy, Gallipoli for blunder. Mons stood for romance. The Canal Bank of Mons, the

Battle of Mons, the Retreat from Mons, the Angels of Mons, the Mons Star, were phrases that caught the public's imagination.

Mons was the first British battle on the continent of Europe since Waterloo, ninety-nine years previously. It was the first time British soldiers had faced Germans since the Anglo-Saxons, Germans themselves, had conquered Roman Britain after the collapse of the Roman Empire. The British had gone to war because of the German invasion of Belgium, and the Battle of Mons was clear evidence that the British army was on the continent, resisting the invader.

The German plan for attacking France was practical and simple. It was suddenly and in strength to attack the French army before its mobilisation was complete, and long before the Russians could come into action to help their French allies. Ten divisions were considered sufficient to keep the Russians occupied on the eastern front, but sixty-two were to be sent against the French. It was the famous Schlieffen Plan drawn up in 1905.

In the west the five right-hand German armies were to be drawn up in line facing west. When mobilisation was complete, they would advance and make a gigantic left wheel, pivoting with the left on Metz and ignoring the neutrality of Belgium. Making a vast sweep west, south-west, south and finally east, the Germans would gather into their net two-thirds of the French army and any British forces encountered. The right-hand German army, under Von Kluck, having 'exterminated the contemptible little British army', was to keep well out to the west and pass round Paris on the north. Then, turning east it was to press the French and British armies up against the line of the fortresses from Verdun to Belfort.

The first check to the great sweep occurred in Belgium, where the Belgian army opposed the advance of the Germans had to be brushed aside and the great forts covering Liège and Namur silenced. All this took some time, and not only gave France several more days for preparation but brought Great Britain into the war, honouring her undertaking to preserve Belgium's neutrality. The Battle of Mons further held up the great sweep, and by 23 August the Germans were already ten days late in their programme.

The British Expeditionary Force crossed the Channel from Southampton and Dublin, disembarking secretly at Boulogne, Le Havre and Rouen. The force consisted of the 1st and 2nd Divisions

(1 Corps) under Sir Douglas Haig, 3rd and 5th Divisions and 19th Independent Infantry Brigade (2 Corps) under Sir Horace Smith-Dorrien, and a cavalry division of five brigades under Sir Edmund Allenby.

Of the three great armies about to face each other, the British was by far the most experienced. The men in the ranks had an average of five years' regular service, while most of the reservists in the ranks called back to the colours in August had during their Regular service served overseas in the Empire in good and bad climates for seven years. Most officers above the rank of subaltern had Boer War or North-West Frontier of India service, and medals, as had many senior NCOs.

There were no conscripts; all were long-service volunteers, and the men knew when they enlisted in peace-time that their service would probably be for eight years. The officers were pure professionals, 90 per cent having been trained at Sandhurst or Woolwich.

The German army was equally good, though in entirely different ways. Its first outstanding characteristic was its superb equipment, which was better than any other army's in the world. No man or unit lacked for anything, and it was tuned and entirely ready for a campaign on the declaration of war. Secondly it was imbued with a sense of invincibility, not having been turned or driven or even checked since Ligny in 1815. This superiority complex was enhanced by its victorious and ruthless advance across Belgium, which thus quickly became to the Germans conquered enemy territory. Lastly, it was knit by the most rigid discipline ever seen in any army in the World's history. Without such discipline no troops could have attacked in 1914 in solid squares in the face of modern small-arms fire from the most efficient infantrymen in the world. The rigid discipline of the men was matched by the rigid thinking of the officers, who practised these tactics of Napoleon's Old Guard at Waterloo for some months, suffering fearful casualties.

The French army was yet again different. It lacked the rigid discipline of the Germans and their complete and superb equipment. It lacked the battle experience of the British, with their highly efficient musketry and wonderful regimental esprit de corps. The French were not good in defence or withdrawal, being easily depressed; but in a successful advance their élan was even better than that of the Australians three years later.

The French army had glamour. A great military history of world-shaking victories, and defeats, was based on the tradition of a leader – Napoleon, perhaps the 'Greatest Captain in History' – dead only just over ninety years. Strategically and tactically its generals, educated at the most brilliant staff college in Europe, were considered to be the best theoretical and thinking tacticians in the three armies. It had yet another great driving force – revenge. It was determined to wipe out the disgrace of the defeats of 1870, and by throwing the hated invader off the soil of France show that Gravelotte and Sedan had only been chance victories for the Germans.

There stood the three armies, each superior to the other two in different ways. It was to be a battle between giants.

The British moved forward from the ports by train as far as Le Cateau, and thence marched across the Belgian frontier to Mons. These five days of marching on the extremely rough and uncomfortable pavé roads in very hot weather was a great trial for the recalled reservists, and most battalions had many men falling out. However, the novelty of the scene and situation, the welcome from the villagers, the cheap and often free food, fruit, and wine, made sore feet less and less important as the advance progressed, and by the time Mons was reached on 22 August, the men were very fit.

The town of Mons, surrounded by a tangle of small coalmining villages, numberless coal tips, and narrow streets and lanes, was at the centre of the line taken up by the BEF. To the south-east of the town 1 Corps, with both 1st and 2nd Divisions up, each with two brigades forward, covered a front of 7 miles facing slightly north of east. Its left forward battalion, The South Staffords, joined hands with the Royal Scots, the right-hand battalion of 2 Corps at the village of Harmignies, 4 miles south-east of Mons; 2 Corps lined the canal bank running westward from the town.

That corps was attacked on its 15-mile frontage by three German corps and three cavalry divisions, whose superiority of force was more than three to one. The massive advance was detected early in the morning of 23 August by aeroplanes of the Royal Flying Corps. It was the first time aircraft had ever been used on active

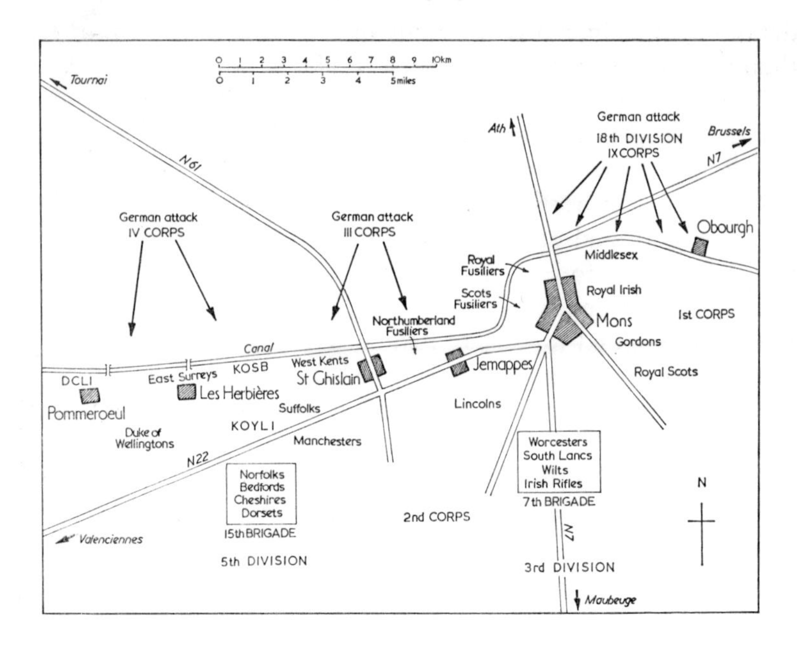

service, and although the news brought was alarming, aerial reconnaissance was not treated very seriously for some days.

The 3rd Division held the broad 1½-mile salient the canal makes as it almost circles the town, and the Middlesex and Royal Fusiliers, the two battalions holding the north-east and north segments, had a very rough time. The 18th German Division crossed the canal on either side of the Middlesex, who were attacked on their front and on both flanks. The battalion called for support from the Royal Irish on their right rear, which was instantly given, but the overwhelming numerical superiority of the enemy prevailed, and the battalion eventually had to withdraw for 1½ miles, having suffered 400 casualties. On their left the Royal Fusiliers also had a bad time, withdrawing late in the afternoon through the town of Mons. They too had heavy casualties, losing 300 men killed and wounded but gaining two VCs, one of which was won by the machine-gun officer.

About an hour after the Middlesex had been attacked, and on the western-facing segment of the salient and thence along the canal, the Scots Fusiliers and the Northumberland Fusiliers were also heavily attacked. However, their fire positions were excellent, the enemy in full view in their advancing squares made superb targets and the British soldiers did great execution. Few of the enemy reached the British-held side of the canal bank, and in this area the British defensive tactics were rewarded with a great victory.

The Northumberland Fusiliers suffered through their chivalry. One party of Germans, having been repulsed by the infantry fire, tried again, this time driving a party of little Belgian schoolgirls down a lane in front of them. The Fusiliers naturally held their fire and the Germans, taking advantage of this, rushed the lock gates and crossed the canal, threatening seriously both Fusilier companies concerned. It was the beginning of the infiltration, and the first instance of 'not playing the game', which was to infuriate the British soldiers.

Further along the canal the ground opposite the West Kents and the KOSB (King's Own Scottish Borderers) near St Ghislain was 'closer', with numerous kitchen gardens, hedges, barbed wire fences, small clumps of trees and chicken huts breaking the lines of advance. These obstacles, however, were of little hindrance to the enemy, who circumnavigated them by rigid 'changing of direction' by word of command from the German battalion or company commanders mounted on perfectly trained horses. The tactics were little more than battalion drill on rough ground. The footbridges over the canal and the lock gates were, of course, closely covered, but despite the defensive fire, some were crossed by small and very gallant parties of the enemy. Unable to advance far over the canal, the Germans nevertheless became of great nuisance value to the defending battalions, sometimes infiltrating between them and sometimes between companies, and several short withdrawals had to be made.

Further to the west along the canal the East Surreys and the DCLI (Duke of Cornwall's Light Infantry) at Les Herbières and Pommeroeul respectively had similar superb targets, but by sheer weight of numbers the enemy reached the north bank of the canal. The West Kents and KOSBs each had two companies on the far side, but all had to withdraw by the lock gates. The East Surreys were attacked by a German regiment of two battalions, which was shot to pieces, the British battalion suffering only a handful of casualties.

Altogether it was a good morning's work for 2 Corps. Smith-Dorrien's 3rd and 5th Divisions and 19th Brigade had held off four German Divisions. Indeed only eleven battalion had been seriously engaged by early afternoon, while on the right Haig's 1 Corps had been largely untroubled.

However, about 3 pm the Germans mounted another major attack on the Mons salient. Again tremendous casualties were caused by the British fire, but the enemy had by now crossed the canal in force and almost surrounded the Middlesex in their second position. Again the Royal Irish went to their help, though enemy shrapnel fire made advance very difficult. By 3.30 pm both these units had to withdraw from their eastern segment of the salient, the Royal Fusiliers at its tip having already started to move back through the town.

The whole line began a simultaneous withdrawal. It was not ordered by the Commander-in-Chief or either of the two corps commanders. It was not organised or coordinated. It was a withdrawal to better positions nearby, and was carried out by company, battalion, and brigade commanders all acting in concert though without cooperation. It was a remarkable example of a number of professionals all trained in the same school acting similarly, sensibly and simultaneously.

Two days previously Sir John French had visited the French Fifth Army commander, General Lanrezac. They had agreed that neither the French Fifth Army nor the BEF should make a withdrawal of any importance without informing the other. Until 5 pm Sir John had received no indication whatever of any intended withdrawal on his right and, knowing that his two corps were holding the enemy, felt not unpleased with the general situation. But in the late evening he received very serious news regarding the French Fifth Army.

On Lanrezac's right the French Fourth Army had suffered severe casualties, and two of its corps had been compelled to retire. This frightened Lanrezac and he too decided to withdraw; but he omitted to inform Sir John of the retirement of his army, which had already started. By the time news of this French retirement had been very carefully considered at British GHQ, and an obvious decision made that a big and general withdrawal was unavoidable, it was nearly midnight.

By 9 pm all the battalions had left the Canal and in the dark were finding their way, and frequently losing it, through the tangle of mining villages, slagheaps, and winding lanes. The men were very tired, quite certain that no retirement was necessary. By dawn all were on the move again, many men, especially transport drivers, getting little more than an hour's sleep.

The Battle of Mons was very largely a musketry and machine-gun battle between efficient Regular soldiers. It lasted only ten hours, engaged only two and a half British divisions, totalling 35,000 men, and cost 1,600 British casualties. The Germans, in their concentrated dark grey squares, advancing against this devastating small-arms fire astounded the British regimental officers and men, who marvelled at the enemy discipline, bravery and foolishness. The Scots Fusiliers and the Northumberland Fusiliers, both flanks guarded, could hardly believe it all to be true.

Two important facts emerged from the battle. Firstly, the British soldiers, although very tired, were in high spirits. They had met the most renowned army in the world and given a good account of themselves. They thought the traditional superiority, born at Crécy, of British soldiers over 'foreigners' was yet again proved.

Secondly, and very important, was the fact that the German advance according to the Schlieffen Plan, already ten days behind schedule, was delayed yet another day. The British army had avoided a considerable chance of encirclement and had slipped away into the night. An iron curtain came down behind it, leaving the enemy breathless, bewildered, badly mauled – but victorious? The Battle of Mons was over, the Retreat from Mons was about to begin.

Until the late 1960s the Canal at Mons was still in use. Today it is being dammed into sections and then drained. The steep sides are being more gradually sloped, so that along the bottom may be laid an 'Auto-Route', the existing bridges remaining as flyovers. The lane down which the little Belgian girls were driven towards the Northumberland Fusiliers is still there, opposite Jemappes. Many of the old buildings from 1914 remain, mostly in ruins. Their use as company headquarters, or OPs for the gunners, must have been widespread.

In the centre of the DCLIs position, just south of Pommeroeul around the bridge carrying the important road from Bavai to

Leuze across the canal, there is much work going on. A new bridge with a considerable embankment is being built here and much of the excavated soil is being used. A large heap of this soil, examined in October 1969, contained two shell splinters from German guns searching for the bridge in 1914.

In 1964, on the north side of the canal and in the area whence the two outpost companies of the 1st Royal West Kents were driven back, the author picked up the remains of a British rifle in the corner of a ploughed field. All the woodwork had long since rotted away, the bolt action was rusted solid and the barrel was completely filled with soil. No other military equipment or debris was found nearby, and it is probable that a soldier retreating hurriedly back to the canal bank in the face of pursuing Uhlans was badly wounded. His friends, already heavily laden in their marching order, carried him back across the canal, leaving the rifle behind them.

In the town museum at Mons, part of the Hôtel de Ville, one room, is devoted entirely to 23 August 1914. Among many relics are four side drums from different regiments and the bass drum of the 2nd Manchesters, who were in reserve to the west of Mons. A collection of cap badges of those regiments that fought at Mons is on display.

13 Le Cateau: 1914

SITE *From Le Cateau along the N39 Cambrai road.*
CONTESTANTS *The British 2nd Army Corps, comprising the 3rd, 4th and 5th Divisions, 19th Independent Brigade, and three Cavalry Brigades, totalling 60,000 men, with 120 guns, under the command of Lt-Gen Sir Horace Smith-Dorrien; and four German army corps and one German cavalry division, with 180 guns.*
CASUALTIES *British killed and badly wounded amounted to 7,800, and nearly 4,000 prisoners and 38 guns were lost. The numbers of German killed and wounded are not known, but probably amounted to 15,000, owing to the extremely accurate British rifle and machine-gun fire. They lost only a handful of field guns by British counter-battery fire, and less than 100 prisoners.*
NOTE *Le Cateau was the last great battle in military history to be fought within the space of one day.*

PRESENT ACCOMMODATION *There is no suitable hotel in Le Cateau. In Cambrai, 12 miles to the north-west, Hôtels Poste and Mouton Blanc are adequate for one night.*

During the Battle of Mons on 23 August Sir John French, the British Commander-in-Chief, learnt two disturbing facts. Firstly, there was a large force of German cavalry out on his exposed left flank, and secondly, that the French Fifth Army on his right had withdrawn without informing him, although there was an agreement between him and the French Commander to keep each other fully informed of major moves. Clearly Sir John, although having just won the Battle of Mons, must now carry out a massive and lengthy withdrawal. He selected a line 30 miles to his rear, in the vicinity of Le Cateau, but the increasing speed of the French Fifth Army's retreat made him change his mind and continue to fall back.

The 2nd British Corps, under Sir Horace Smith-Dorrien, had taken the brunt of the massive enemy attacks at Mons on 23 August and on the evening of the 25th was wearily trudging through Le Cateau. Sir Horace's three divisional commanders, and the cavalry commander, all told him that the men and horses were too exhausted to march on through the night. Accordingly he took the decision to ignore French's order to continue the retreat, and to stand and fight next day. The right of the line was to include Le Cateau, while the left would lie near Haucourt, some 5 miles due west. The next day, 26 August, was the anniversary of Crécy.

On the extreme right of the whole line, the Duke of Cornwall's Light Infantry of the 5th Division, not having yet received the orders to stand and fight, were forming up in fours on the Le Cateau road preparatory to continuing the retreat, when they were fired on from the windows of the houses lining the north side of the road, and men began to drop. Hurriedly they were moved up to the higher ground farther east, where, with two companies of the East Surreys, they held for some hours the rather weak attack by the German advanced elements around the British right flank.

Looking at the position today it seems unlikely that the DCLI were in fact fired at from these houses, as the official history states. About 70 yards behind these houses, on the enemy side of the road, is a steep bank, almost a cliff, several feet high, and the enemy could have fired down at the DCLI from the cliff top through the gaps between the houses. By wasting time in forcing entry into houses, and climbing stairs, they might well have missed the perfect target of a stationary battalion lined up in fours.

To the immediate west of Le Cateau the KOYLIs (King's Own Yorkshire Light Infantry) and the KOSBs (King's Own Scottish Borderers) were extended about 300 yards south of the main road. On this entirely open and gently sloping forward piece of ground some trenches had been dug by the inhabitants of Le Cateau. It is not known what authority decided on this step, who organised the labour and tools, or who directed the work. It seems an impossible task with the chaos in the town, where most civilians were packing to get away, refugees were pouring in, and every man looking after his own affairs. Yet these trenches were dug. Only 3 feet deep, they were not deep enough, and the two battalions had to use their own entrenching tools to improve them. They afforded some cover, but being on such open ground were very obvious.

B Company of the KOYLI on the right formed a refused right flank along the lesser road running back from the main road. Today it can be seen to have magnificent flank protection, the men lying down behind the road with an excellent field of fire in front.

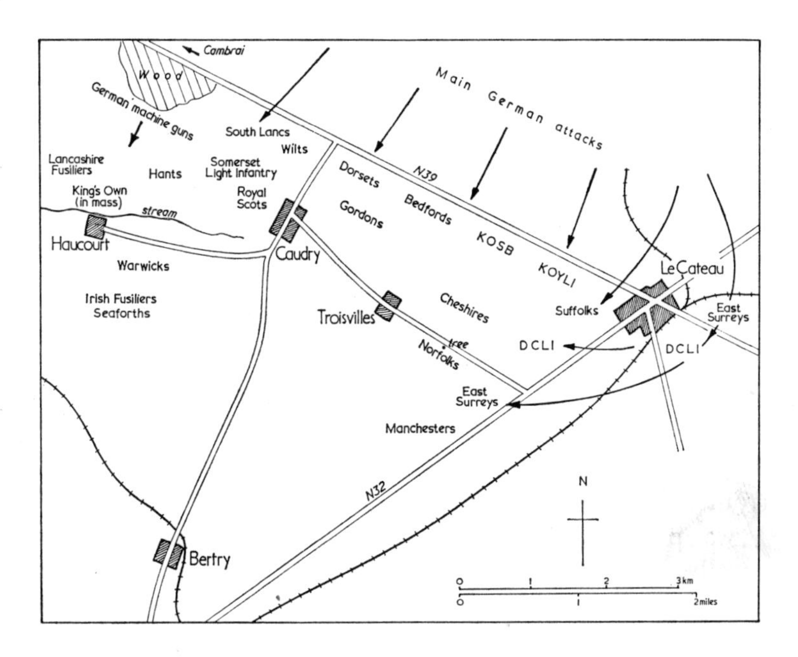

The enemy artillery had, however, a magnificent target in the civilian-sited trenches, and by their fire they greatly helped the German infantry regiments forward in their attack across the main road. The KOYLI suffered severely but, refusing to surrender or withdraw, caused heavy casualties by their musketry and the one remaining machine gun. The enemy naturally hesitated to rush in. Several times their bugles sounded the British 'Cease Fire', and an attempt was made to take forward a flag of truce. Each overture was met by renewed defensive fire, but gradually the enemy got round the flanks. Many now came forward from the front and the remaining men of the KOYLI could not fire fast enough to hold them. Finally some Germans came up behind them, and a close-quarter bayonet and fist fight ensued. Overcome by vastly superior numbers, they were mostly captured, and the battalion, within a few short hours, lost 600 officers and men, the majority being taken prisoner. One of the captured officers, Keppel, was mess president, and had the mess chequebook in his pocket when taken. Some time after arrival in the officers' prisoner-of-war camp, he drew a cheque for £6, each of the twelve captured officers endorsing it for 10s. He managed to bribe a German civilian to cash it, and in due course it reached Cox's Bank for payment, whereupon the bank informed each officer's next-of-kin. It was the first news any of the relatives, or indeed the War Office, had received since before the Battle of Mons. The cheque is still preserved in the Regimental Museum at Beverley.

The brigade to the left of the KOSB consisted of the Norfolks, Bedfords, Cheshires, and Dorsets. It was an entirely ordinary brigade, all regiments being English county regiments. There were no Fusiliers, no Light Infantry, no Highlanders and no Irish regiments. The men were very largely from the country, and were very hard to shift. It was one of the best brigades in the BEF. At Mons it had been in reserve and had not fired a shot, but on the following day, the first day of the Great Retreat, it had been rear-guard to the 5th Division, and the Cheshires had been all but surrounded, losing almost 600 men.

It was put into the centre of the front line at Le Cateau, with, naturally, the Cheshires as its brigade reserve. But there was no serious German pressure before midday and then very little in the centre, and so in two major actions in five days the brigade saw little serious fighting. On its front the ground is slightly more broken than that occupied by the KOSB and KOYLI, and there are low banks, ditches and minor features of tactical value, which the forward companies occupied and from which excellent fields of fire are obtainable.

Eastward, and across the main road here, the ground is very level, and German infantry advancing over it would have suffered severely, in spite of artillery support brought down on the Bedfords and Dorsets holding the front line. However, the Germans did not attack. The headquarters of this brigade were in a sunken lane, with 8-foot banks. Alongside the headquarters were the Norfolks in reserve, digging themselves well into the eastern bank. On the reverse side of the very slight slope that runs back from the main road, they were unable to understand why so many shells were falling so close to them and brigade headquarters in the sunken lane. Clearly both were out of sight of the enemy. However, on top of one of the banks an entirely isolated tree was standing, large enough to be marked on the map and very conspicuous. The Norfolks spent a long time trying to cut it down, but as soon as it was cut half through, so as to fall to the south, the wind, blowing strongly from the south-west, threatened to blow it down to the north and thus into and over the sunken lane. This would have been a disaster indeed, blocking the road wherein much transport was already parked. Having been half cut through, it then had to be guyed up with ropes, but eventually it was brought down on the right side of the sunken road, and the shelling died down considerably.

Today the roots of this great tree are clearly visible. Twenty years ago a sapling was planted among them, which is now half-grown, 20 feet high, and is clearly visible on the bank from a great distance. Its giant predecessor, twice its height, must have been conspicuous indeed, and explains the Germans' interest and attention.

Farther along the line, and now in the 3rd Division's area, the exact positions of the Royal Scots, Gordons and, over the road in front of the town of Caudry, the South Lancs and the Wiltshires, are easily identifiable. This part of the line was heavily attacked throughout the day by cavalry, three infantry regiments (six battalions) and consistent heavy artillery fire. Casualties were considerable. Minor indentations in the line were made but surprisingly were not exploited until nightfall.

At dusk the Corps Commander authorised individual withdrawal by units, but in the 3rd Division this order failed to reach the Gordons. In the fading light they did not see that the South Lancs, the Wiltshires and the Royal Scots were moving back. About 10 pm the CO was wounded, and the second-in-command, who had taken over, noticed the silence all round him and realised that a withdrawal must have taken place. Accordingly he concentrated what was left of the battalion and led them back, hopeful that he was moving in the right direction. After about 4 miles in the dark, complete silence and isolation, he passed through two villages, and then came to a T-junction in the road. Having by now largely lost all sense of direction, he decided to turn left, which led him into the village of Bertry, instead of right, which would have probably allowed him to escape. In the village he saw lights in a cottage and heard voices. Forcing his way into the house, he found it occupied by many German soldiers. Bertry, small and compact, had been captured by the enemy some hours before, and in no time the Gordons were in the midst of an exultant enemy, who surrounded them, capturing all except a handful of men in the rear company who turned and ran.

On reaching the road junction today, and after following the route the Gordons took along the winding lane, it is still necessary, even in broad daylight, to consult the map to establish one's bearings. Standing there it is easy to realise how Major Gordon made his mistake in the dark, even if he had a map, and experience the uncertainty in his mind as he stood at the road junction.

Out on the left flank the 12th Brigade faced north-east, to form a refused flank to any German attempt to come in there. This brigade, although fresh by comparison with those troops who had been in action or marching since the Canal engagement, was nevertheless tired. It had detrained at Le Cateau in the early morning of the 25th after twenty-four hours in the train, and there was not much sleep to be had in the cattle trucks provided. It had been marched forward all day, and taking over the rearguard from the 5th Division, had marched back again, deployed and fought its way all through the night, reaching its position out on the extreme left flank at dawn on the 26th.

The left forward battalion, the Lancashire Fusiliers, started to dig in on high ground north-west of Haucourt, while the right battalion, the King's Own Royal Lancasters, formed mass on the forward slope, piled arms and removed equipment. The men were lying down. It was said that the French cavalry were out in front protecting the brigade.

About 6 am, while most of the King's Own were still asleep, a junior officer reported that he had just seen two or three horsemen ride out from the wood 1,000 yards in front, observe the battalion and then withdraw. He added that their uniforms were foreign.

Little notice was taken until, a little later, a wheeled vehicle left the wood, advanced a hundred yards or so and paused, with much activity. In a few moments machine-gun fire, at a range of 800 yards, opened on the battalion sleeping en masse. In the first burst eighty-three men were killed, including the CO, and over 200 wounded. Men rushed to unpile arms, equipment and ammunition was searched for, and general chaos prevailed. Although the machine-gun fire was quickly and accurately followed by shrapnel fire, the second-in-command was able to rally the battalion and withdraw it 100 yards behind the crest.

Here some reorganisation was possible, and a party was sent forward to engage the enemy, who had by now also withdrawn. The Royal Warwicks from the 10th Brigade (in reserve) came forward to support and later relieve the King's Own, who were withdrawn into reserve at Haucourt.

The exact position of the battalion when surprised can be precisely fixed. The forward open slope continuing evenly downhill for 1,000 yards is very clear, while only 50 yards behind the battalion's position is the crest of the slope and then a sharp drop to the valley of a little stream – an ideal defensive position. To its right there is a slight rise in the ground over which the Hampshires could not been seen. A post on this ridge would have made a link with this unit and also provided further observation over a large area forward. The example of the Lancashire Fusiliers in digging in, clearly seen by the King's Own, should have been followed.

On the map of the Battle of Le Cateau, the position of every infantry battalion at 8 am on the 26th is shown. All but one of those units in the front line, and many in support, were in 'extended order' – digging in, presumably. The exception is the King's Own, and it is surprising that a regular infantry battalion should have been caught unawares, as it was.

The CO of the King's Own, Lt-Col Dykes, had been adjutant of his regiment at Spion Kop in 1900, had in 1902 received a brevet-majority for his work in the South African War, had passed through the Staff College in 1909, and had been in command of the battalion for a year before August 1914. That this obviously able, intelligent and experienced officer should so completely ignore two great principles of war, security and surprise, was a blunder that cost him his life and those of eighty-three of his men.

As the day progressed, the Royal Warwicks and the Lancashire Fusiliers were pressed back towards Haucourt, and by dusk the Royal Warwicks withdrew through the village, the King's Own thus again becoming the right forward battalion of the 12th Brigade. About 8 pm permission to withdraw by units was received, and about the same time the Germans entered the eastern outskirts of Haucourt. Several minor isolated incidents took place in the darkness while the King's Own were preparing to leave, and one officer and several men were killed.

In the village of Haucourt in 1955 one old man still remembered the battle, the disaster to the King's Own, their withdrawal after dark and the German occupation for the next four years. He also remembered as a child seeing the German troops march through in 1870, and a similar invasion in 1940.

Towards evening the enemy artillery fire increased. The villages in or just behind the line, where naturally brigade and battalion headquarters were posted, together with reserve units and services, suffered severely. Both flanks had been turned, and by 6 pm it was evident that the brigades in the centre, although quite undefeated, could not stay much longer without risking being totally surrounded. A complete withdrawal to preserve a line with the retreating flank brigades was inevitable.

By 7 pm dusk was falling, as well as a light drizzle. All the officers and men, not only in the battalion but at brigade and divisional headquarters were very tired, and everyone knew that a ghastly night lay ahead of them, with no rest and probably no food, certainly nothing hot. The men did not grumble – the British soldier never does when times are really bad. The general mood was one of apathy. There were only two alternatives, they believed – this present hell or a good sleep – but they knew they would not get the latter.

As at Mons, 2 Corps slipped away in the dark. The weary troops marched all night, but they suffered little molestation. The enemy had had enough for the time being.

The Battle of Le Cateau, the last great battle to be fought within the space of a day, achieved its object. It gave many men in the reserve battalions and brigades who were not engaged until late in the day several hours of sleep. It hit the enemy a hard blow from which he recoiled, so that he did not again closely pursue or harass the infantry during the Great Retreat; and it allowed 1 Corps to get clear away. Lastly it delayed the programme of the German advance by yet another day. It had been already ten days late at Mons, owing to the resistance of the Belgian forts of Namur and Liége. Mons put it back another day, while Le Cateau added yet another.

The success of the Schlieffen Plan depended on adherence to a strict timetable, so that the Western Allies could be knocked out by a certain date and then the bulk of the German army transferred to the east to meet the Russians before their mobilisation was complete. Every day lost on this rigid, typically German, programme was a day gained for Russia. The resistance shown by 2 Corps at Le Cateau contributed towards that end.

Nevertheless, despite its satisfactory long-term result, the Battle of Le Cateau, wherein an advancing enemy in great strength pushed a British corps of three divisions off its semi-prepared position, forcing it to retreat through the night, can hardly be termed a British victory. Yet the words 'Le Cateau' appear on the Colours as a battle honour of all the regiments who took part. Quatre Bras in 1815, however, where an attacking enemy (also in strength) was repulsed by the British and forced to withdraw into the night, is not considered a victory and its name appears on no Colours.

14 Ypres: 1914–15, 1917

SITE *Ypres lies on the main road, N9, Dunkirk to Brussels, about 25 miles south-east of Dunkirk.*

CONTESTANTS 1st Ypres – *1st British Corps of three divisions and one cavalry division under General Haig, about 35,000 men, against the 4th German Army of three army corps.*

2nd Ypres – *1st British Army of four divisions, of 40,000 men under General Haig, against three German corps of about 90,000.*

Passchendaele – *The 5th British Army, under General Gough, and part of the 2nd Army, General Plumer, totalling on the opening day, 31 July 1917, perhaps 100,000 men. By the end of the battle in November, however, all but nine of the fifty-nine British infantry divisions in France had taken some part in the battle, usually two periods of two weeks each. The battle lasted three and a half months.*

CASUALTIES *A remotely approximate figure is difficult to estimate. On the Memorial Arch at the Menin Gate at Ypres there are the names of 65,000 missing men who have no known grave. The largest British cemetery has 12,000 graves. Probably 100,000 officers and men were killed or died of wounds in the four years, apart from the 65,000 missing. The German casualties would probably be greater, owing to their practice of attacking in mass in 1914.*

PRESENT ACCOMMODATION *There are two or three quite good hotels which cater especially for one-or-two night visitors. Dinner is arranged to finish in time for leaving for the Menin Gate nightly ceremony of the 'Last Post'. Taxis are plentiful and the drivers know the district well, speaking quite good English. Many of them are third generation, whose family has made the profession a traditional occupation.*

Ypres is very near the centre of the Cockpit of Europe. The name, of course, conjures up memories of the two battles of the old city in 1914 and 1915 and the Battle of Passchendaele in 1917, but Ypres has been the scene of military events for almost 600 years, since 1395, when a British force under the Bishop of Norwich laid siege to the city. The siege was lifted on the approach of a large French army, and to this day the relief from this siege is commemorated by a small annual festival.

In the fourteenth century Ypres, with a population of over 200,000, was the largest city in Flanders. As a result it became the meeting place of seven important roads and a canal, later to be joined by two railway lines. But long before 1914 the importance of Ypres had greatly dwindled and by that year its population was barely 20,000. It was still the junction of seven roads, however, and had retained the strategic importance it had enjoyed during the centuries. Through it passed the Duke of Palma in 1745, when the city with several others passed to France under the Second Treaty of Versailles. The Austrians, and Marlborough with his Redcoats, had been there. In 1870 some outlying Prussian cavalry scouts had passed nearby on their way to Paris, after Sedan. In 1940 Ypres saw the withdrawal of the British army to Dunkirk, and in 1944 Montgomery's 21st Army Group toured through on its way from Normandy to the Baltic. But it was in World War I that Ypres became such a household word.

After the Battle of the Aisne, following the Retreat from Mons and the Battle of the Marne, the British army was pulled out of the trench line and moved up to the extreme left flank of the Allied forces, to protect the Channel ports. It naturally held Ypres and its great road junction, taking up a position around a great semicircle with a radius of 5 miles out from the town. Its right segment was extended south of the town for 10 miles, where the British line made contact with the French forces, while its northern limit met the Belgian army near Nieuport.

On 18 October 1914 the Germans made the first of their two great attempts to capture Ypres. They had not fully learned their lesson from the canal bank at Mons, or from Le Cateau, and were still practising the very costly method of attacking in mass against a well-trained army of expert riflemen. For nearly three weeks their repeated attacks were repulsed with heavy losses. Indeed the

British riflemen and machine gunners sometimes could not fire fast enough to halt advances and would succeed only in slowing them down. There was a gradual contraction of the great semi-circular salient, and as the line got shorter, it also got thinner.

The northern half of the salient was held by the 1st and 2nd Divisions, and the southern segment by the 7th Division. The latter covered Gheluvelt on the Menin Road, and the two cavalry divisions, recently formed and acting as infantry, extended the line west and south-west.

The weight of the German attacks from 18 October fell mainly on the 7th Division astride the Menin Road, running south-east from Ypres. On 31 October Gheluvelt was lost and the division had now been pushed back over a mile to its right rear. That afternoon the South Wales Borderers, of the 1st Division on the left of the 7th and holding the grounds of Gheluvelt Château, came under extreme pressure. A fresh German regiment had been brought forward, and, after several attacks, had almost isolated the battalion from its respective neighbours, the Queen's and the Welch Regiment. Away to the right the Scots Guards, down to 200 men, were barely holding on, and it seemed that the line must break. If so,

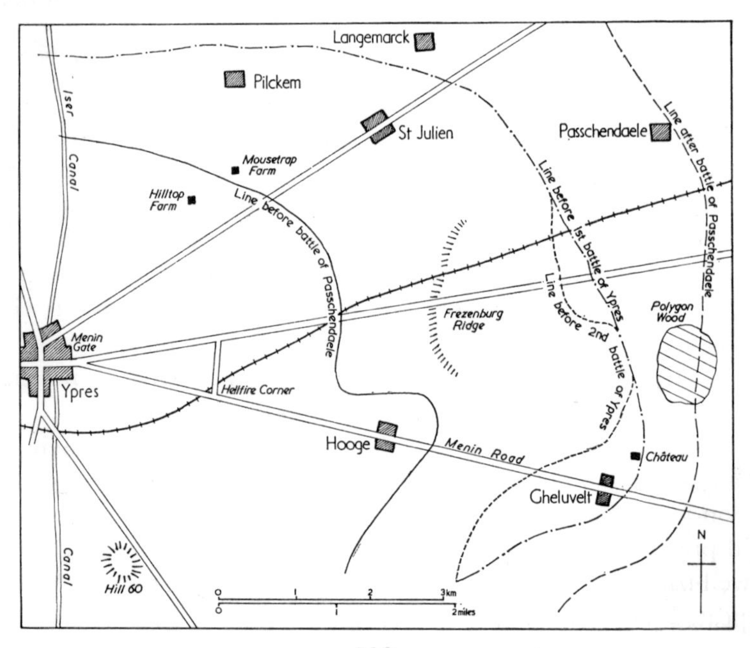

the Germans would have passed through the 1st Division and thereby outflanked, overrun and defeated the BEF. The way to the Channel ports would have been open.

The 2nd Worcesters from the 2nd Division were in reserve in Polygon Wood, a mile away. They were ordered to advance across open ground to reinforce the South Wales Borderers and prevent the imminent capture of Gheluvelt Château. For the first 600 yards the battalion was under cover of woods on their left, but on reaching Polderhoek Château they had to cross open country, and for 1,000 yards there was no cover of any sort. Over 100 men were killed or wounded out of 400, but the battalion pressed on until they reached Gheluvelt Château, there joining the South Wales Borderers. Some of the men, with the bit between their teeth, carried on into the village, where they found some Germans in a ruined cottage cooking for their battalion. The cooks, though in superior numbers, were so surprised that they turned and ran, while the few Worcesters returned to the Château. The charge of the Worcesters at Gheluvelt was perhaps the finest exploit of any single battalion in the whole of World War I. It can only be challenged by the 1st Lancashire Fusiliers in their original landing on the Gallipoli Peninsula, when the battalion earned six Victoria Crosses in one day.

A mile behind the front line at Gheluvelt and on the Menin Road stands the village of Hooge, with its château. Both the 1st and 2nd Divisions had their headquarters in the château during the battle, where disaster occurred on 1 November, the day after the Worcesters' charge. About 2 pm a low-flying enemy aeroplane evidently saw vehicles, staff officers holding maps, and horses, all congregated in the grounds of the château. Among them were the two divisional commanders, Generals Monro and Lomax, with their GSOs I and II. A few minutes after the aircraft had flown away four shells burst on the château. The second shell fell on the assembled staff, General Lomax being so badly wounded that he died in England later. All four staff officers were killed, and General Monro badly stunned, although after treatment he was able to carry on.

Ten days later the persistent German attacks ceased. There was little hope of breaking through the British lines, and the enormous casualties they had suffered seemed too big a price to pay for the capture of the town. A third reason was the appalling mud that made mobility almost impossible.

The only tactical result of the three-week attempt by the Germans to break through had been the restriction of the semi-circle round the town. By 11 November it was only 11 miles in circumference instead of the original 16 and its radius had shrunk from 5 miles to 3½.

Today Gheluvelt Château has been rebuilt, but the lawn in front of the house where the Worcesters joined the SWBs is still there. Lawn and building can be seen from the main gate but visitors are not welcome. Hooge Château, too, where the generals were shelled, has been rebuilt but on a different plan. It is now a roadhouse, where in the summer the coloured umbrellas over the tables in the garden and waitresses in brightly coloured dresses seem incongruous to the historian. The Menin Road running through Gheluvelt was utterly destroyed by shellfire in the four years 1914–18, but is now rebulit and widened, with the few curves straightened out; today it carries a steady fast-moving stream of cars and lorries. It is one of the most striking examples of the reconstruction that has occurred on the Western Front since 1919.

One of the most unhealthy spots in the salient was Hellfire Corner, where the Zillebeke–Potijze road met the Ypres–Menin road and where a railway track also crossed the road. Hereabouts the ground is largely pasture, and all war debris has been overgrown by grass and sucked into the soil. Yet this pasture seems suspiciously uneven. The many indentations around the crossroads are evidence of shellholes.

A little further down the Menin road Maple Avenue runs off to the right to Maple Copse, where the great Canadian cemetery lies. Just beyond the cemetery there is a small area about 100 yards by 50 yards, much grown over by young trees. Within this enclosure lies a portion of the German front line as it was before 31 July 1917, when the Battle of Passchendaele started. It has escaped the obliteration of the years. The trenches, with softening outlines, are quite clear, the siting and fields of fire show that they are genuine and professional, while the debris and relics in the undergrowth are clearly originals.

Throughout the winter of 1914–15 Ypres was quiet by Great War standards. Only an occasional trench raid interrupted the general state of boredom and acute discomfort. But on 22 April 1915 the Germans made another attempt to capture the town, precipitating the Second Battle of Ypres.

In defiance of the Hague Convention of 1899, totally unexpectedly, and for the first time in history, the attackers used poison gas. The main gas attack came against the north-east segment of the semicircle around Ypres, near the village of Langemarck and Pilckem. Here the line was held by the 1st Canadian Division and, on their left, a French division. The gas was closely followed up by German infantrymen.

The Canadians were badly shaken but the French division broke, and a gap of over 2,000 yards was created. The Germans poured into the gap but were temporarily held by flanking fire from the Canadians, and a fresh British division made a line 200 yards back to which the Canadians conformed. The Germans continued to attack and eventually a massive withdrawal was necessary, reducing the front held by the defending Allies from 20,000 yards to 15,000 and bringing it 1,400 yards nearer to Ypres. Pressure was kept up by the Germans but strong defence by the British held, and by 7 May the salient was again fairly quiet. But on 8 May the most easterly segment of the salient burst into flames again.

The line was held by the 27th and 28th Divisions, both consisting of Regular army battalions brought home from India after relief by certain selected Territorial battalions. These Regular regiments were of superb quality, for all their men were serving soldiers (there were no recalled reservists) with an average of four years in the army, and all were inured to hardship, separation from home and bad climate. These units, in fact, were better than the original battalions at Mons and Le Cateau.

At the extreme point of the salient, and astride the Ypres–Zonnebeke road, ran the Frezenburg Ridge. 'Ridge' is but a courtesy title, for the ground, some 500 yards long and 100 yards wide, is only a few feet above the surrounding country. Immediately in front of the Ridge lies the hamlet of Frezenburg, 50 yards beyond which was the enemy front line.

On the evening of 7 May two private soldiers of the 2nd King's Own went out from the front line to bring in a gate they had seen, to repair the revetment of their trench. In the dark they lost themselves, and wandered towards a small wood where they heard many German voices. On return they reported what they had heard, suggesting that a big attack was imminent. No notice was taken, but the two men were right.

The Germans, knowing the high quality of these two British divisions and determined to obliterate them, attacked with three corps next morning. The battle began with an intense bombardment, much of which was shrapnel, a particularly effective weapon against trenches that in those days had no head cover.

By 8 am the front trenches were virtually flat, with parapets gone and machine guns knocked out. The Germans lifted their bombardment on to the reserve and support lines and then advanced, easily capturing the smashed and almost undefended front line. The few unwounded men alive were quickly captured, the enemy having little difficulty in advancing almost to battalion headquarters, where an 'SOS party' held them up by rapid fire.

There was a nasty gap in the line but the Germans failed to exploit it, and in the afternoon a Territorial battalion, the 5th King's Own Royal Lancasters, counterattacked and partially filled the gap. That night the remnants of the defending troops were relieved.

The King's Own lost, from all causes, fifteen officers, including four killed, and 890 men, many of whom were missing. In the Battle of Le Cateau (see p 107) the other battalion of the King's Own suffered disaster, so that in these two actions, taking but a few hours, the regiment lost over 1,000 officers and men, all of them Regulars. About 500 were taken prisoner.

For over two years after the German attack at Frezenburg Ridge the Ypres Salient was calm, but calm only when compared with Loos, the Somme, or Vimy Ridge. Then on 31 July 1917 a great British offensive was launched on a thirteen-divisional front.

In contrast to the Battle of the Somme, which was fought for its first six weeks in July and August 1916 in hot dry weather, with its accompaniment of flies, dust, and revolting smells in the smashed trenches, the Battle of Passchendaele became synonymous with rain, which started to fall on the already heavy muddy ground twelve hours after the attack started. There were no flies or dust, but such mud as no man had ever seen before.

On the opening day of the Battle of the Somme only six of the thirteen divisions taking part had succeeded in penetrating the enemy lines and holding their gains. At Passchendaele, as the Third Battle of Ypres came to be called, all thirteen divisions succeeded in capturing and retaining enemy front-line trenches, in several cases moving well inside their lines. The reason for this success was twofold. Firstly, the lessons for preparing a large-scale attack, learnt on the Somme, had been applied on 31 July 1917. Secondly, the Germans, who had suffered heavy casualties on the Somme, both material and moral, had recently lost Vimy Ridge to the British in the Battle of Arras and eight weeks later had been driven off Messines Ridge. The cumulative effect of these setbacks was quite apparent on 31 July.

On this opening day at Passchendaele no division advanced less than 600 yards, some considerably more, and the 8th Division finished the day over a mile from its original front line. The enemy had had a bad reverse and was much shaken, whereas the victorious British divisions, with comparatively few casualties compared with those of the first day of the Battle of the Somme, were ready for another advance. They would undoubtedly have had a great success if they had been able to advance again on 1 or 2 August. But about 5 pm on 31 July it started to rain. It rained all night and all the next day, and for several days and nights. In six hours the whole area became a bog – largely caused by the complete breaking-up of the ground by the heavy and incessant shellfire of several days. All the ditches and field drains had been smashed, and the water could not get away. Shellholes filled with water, and twenty-four hours after zero hour on the 31st movement was brought to a virtual standstill.

A brief spell of fine weather intervened, but the rain then returned. For the next three months all advances in the great offensive were but minor affairs, each of a little local or tactical importance but no more.

On the opening day of the great attack farmhouses, copses, slight rises in the ground (which are very rare and barely perceptible) were all of major tactical importance. Although obvious targets for the enemy artillery and thus to be avoided, they formed essential objectives for the British infantry after it had carried the German front-line trenches. All were smashed to pieces by the intense preparatory bombardment but they were still recognisable as features on the ground. After 1918 all these features were restored and mostly stand today. The farmers usually welcome visitors, who are at liberty to take, as souvenirs, items from the little dump of war debris brought in from the fields and still being turned up by the plough today. Tin helmets, parts of rifles, masses of shell splinters from perhaps an inch to a couple of feet long, bayonets, waterbottles, petrol cans, all rusty but recognisable, will be found in each farm's dump. In 1967 the author found, near Mousetrap Farm (close to the Ypres–St Julien road), the vague outline of a huge shellhole in which he had been given first aid on the afternoon of 31 July fifty years earlier.

Every visitor to Ypres should go to the Menin Gate in the evening. At 8 pm in the winter and 9 pm in the summer an impressive little ceremony takes place here. At two minutes before the hour two Belgian gendarmes appear, one at each end of the long arch forming the Gate. They face inward and, extending an arm, hold up all traffic behind them. Carrying silver bugles, two men wearing mackintoshes and berets with the silver badge of the Ypres Fire Brigade appear from among the passers-by and take post in the middle of the now empty roadway. All traffic, movement and noise stop. On the hour the two buglers sound the Last Post. Everyone is silent, all men standing to attention with hats off, and as the notes die away, the silence is almost audible. The buglers, then the gendarmes, break off and mingle with the spectators. Traffic flows again. Life goes on. Apart from the German occupation of 1940 to 1945, this ceremony has never been omitted whatever the weather.

15 Loos: 1915

SITE *Three miles north of Lens on the Lens–La Bassée road, and 12 miles north of Arras on the N347.*
CONTESTANTS *The British First Army under Haig had two corps (eleven divisions), totalling some 100,000 infantrymen. The Germans had five divisions holding the line on the opening day to oppose the leading British divisions. Numbers were approximately equal.*
CASUALTIES *The British lost 1,712 officers and 41,000 other ranks killed, wounded or missing. The Germans lost 440 officers and 19,000 men.*

PRESENT ACCOMMODATION *None recommended in Lens, Loos or Béthune. Arras, 12 miles away, and Lille, 16 miles, each have one or two good hotels. Taxis easily obtainable, and at fair prices. Roads good, but many mining villages.*

In World War I Loos was the first planned and organised attack against a strong dug-in position protected by wire.

Haig had six divisions in line with no reserve, but he kept two divisions, the 21st and 24th, as his own reserve. These divisions comprised men of Kitchener's Army and had existed for less than a year. Few of the men in the ranks or the junior officers had more than twelve month's service, and it seems unwise of the C-in-C to have selected two such inexperienced divisions as the main reserve. If called for, they would be used in open warfare behind the enemy lines, operations demanding skill, training and experience.

Haig's six divisions, left to right, were the 2nd (Regulars), the 9th (Scottish), the 7th (Regular), the 1st (Regular), the 15th

(Scottish) and lastly, on the extreme right, the 47th (London) Territorial.

The two Scottish divisions, composed of both Highland and Lowland battalions, were of superb quality. All the units of the 9th had rather more than a year of growing together. This division was the subject of the famous novel *The First Hundred Thousand* by Ian Hay, who was an officer in the 10th Argyll and Sutherland Highlanders. The 15th was equally good and only a few weeks younger than the 9th.

The last division, the 47th, was also of great quality. Nearly all the men, Londoners, had been in the Territorials for two or three years before the war and were largely of officer material. The mistake of using the battalions of this division, which included the London Scottish, Civil Service Rifles, the Queen's Westminsters, etc, as ordinary infantry, and thus knocking out many potential officers, was not repeated in World War II.

The ground over which the six divisions were to attack was entirely flat. The enemy's line ran in front of several small coal-mining villages, among which appeared great coaltips, known as *crassiers*. The La Bassée Canal out on the left flank was about 40 yards wide and 6 feet deep. Towards the southern edge of the enemy's line stood the town of Loos, with a population of 5,000 people. It was entirely a coalmining town, with numberless coal-tips and towers for operating the shafts and winding gear. It was the objective for the 15th Division, while the 47th Division on its right was to capture the southern suburbs, and especially the Double Crassier, a gigantic coal tip. Behind this crassier stood a very high metal tower for the winding gear of a mine, christened by the Londoners 'Tower Bridge'.

In April 1915 at the Second Battle of Ypres the Germans had sprung the greatest surprise of the war in using poison gas against the defending infantry. Ten days after its first use by the Germans Kitchener had ordered the preparation of retaliatory measures. These were ready in time for Loos and were used by the two corps on the opening day.

The gas was far from effective. The morning was dead calm and the gas refused to drift towards the German lines, as it should have, according to the meteorological experts. The attacking troops had to advance through it, suffering many gas casualties as a result, and in the case of the Oxford and Bucks and the Queens on the extreme left, the faintest zephyr of a wind actually blew some of the gas back on to the reserve companies. In addition to gas the attack was preceded by a four-day bombardment by 530 guns.

The brigade of the 2nd Division on the north of La Bassée Canal had little success. The enemy, strongly entrenched, fought bravely and the gas, made worse by the smoke barrage, caused most sub-units to lose direction. Three hours after zero the brigade was back in its old front line. On the right of the canal, the centre brigade fared little better. Its objective was a group of strongly fortified brick stacks, a position which, with its right flank protected by the canal, could only be assaulted along the tow-path. Naturally the towpath was covered by enemy machine-gun fire, but the South Staffords got forward somehow, almost up to the enemy wire, 300 hundred yards away. Captain Kilby of C Company, although wounded slightly, led his troops gallantly along the path, and when finally badly wounded, used a rifle. He was eventually reported 'wounded and missing', being awarded a posthumous VC. Along the towpath today the site of his death is where the rail line from Vermelles to La Bassée joins that from La Bassée to Béthune.

The left brigade of the next division, the 9th, had a severe repulse. The 6th KOSB and 10th HLI (Highland Light Infantry) advanced slowly almost up to the German wire. Here many men fell into a deep, totally unsuspected trench whose bottom was studded with pointed stakes and festooned with barbed wire, over which its original turves had been relaid on a thin sheet. Men who fell in could scarcely extricate themselves and the two battalions became disorganised. This simple and legitimate defensive work was similar to that employed by Bruce at Bannockburn 600 years previously.

However, the right brigade of the 9th had a great success. Its objective was an unnamed collection of cottages surrounding the end of the railway at a pithead, the whole dominated by a small coal tip, Fosse 8. The British bombardment had badly smashed the buildings and installations, and no greater moonscape could be imagined. However, the two forward battalions, the 5th Camerons, led by Lochiel himself, and the 7th Seaforths, had an immediate

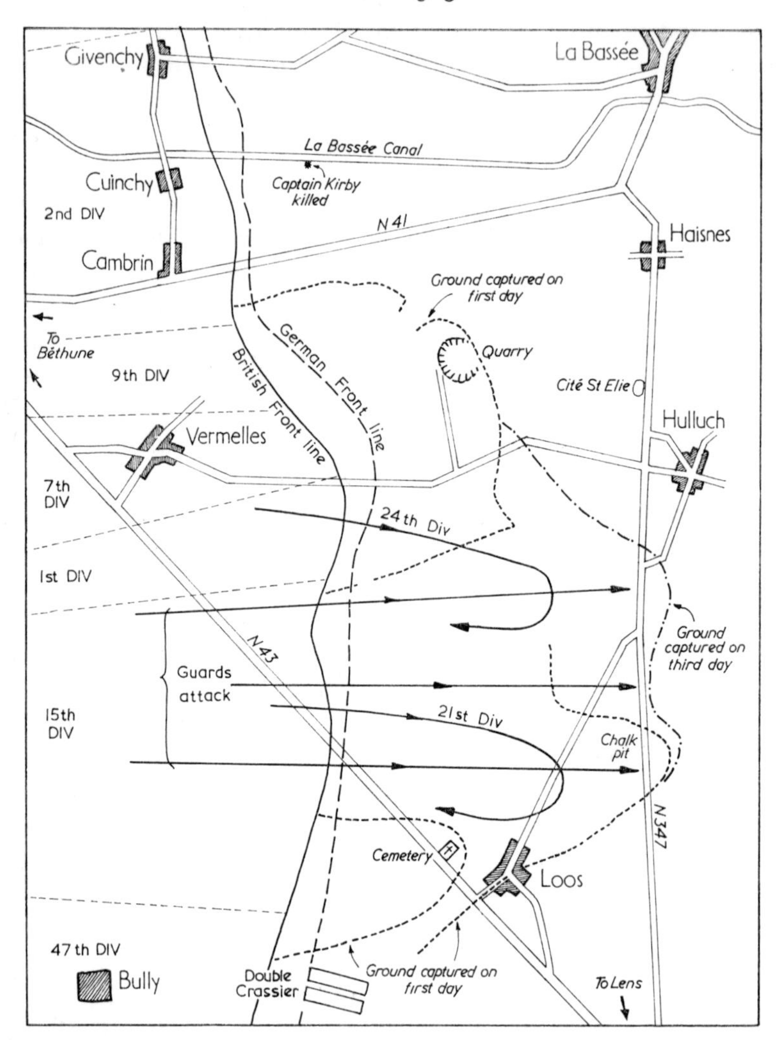

success, and in their first rush captured Fosse 8, half a mile inside the enemy front line. The heavy bombardment of the unnamed village, where the crash and reverberations of the shells on the buildings and the flying brickwork greatly lowered the morale of the defenders, caused the Germans to remain behind cover until too late.

The next division, the 7th, attacked on a 1,200-yard frontage. Neither of the two forward brigades had a tactical feature to capture, the enemy trench lines being the objectives. These two brigades almost reached the German wire. Here the men were to lie down to take a breather, and each man was to select the exact spot in the enemy's wire through which he could penetrate. On a whistle blast all ranks again rushed forward and, clearing the wire, captured the enemy's front-line trench.

In the left brigade the 2nd Royal Warwicks were badly held up, but the Welsh Fusiliers passed through them, while the Queens passed through the South Staffords, and elements of all four battalions captured a large quarry. Moving on, they reached the western edges of the two villages astride the main Lens–La Bassée road, Hulluch and Cité St Elie, three-quarters of a mile beyond their starting line. Brigade HQ came up and established itself in the quarry, and elements of three battalions, the Queens, South Staffords and now the Green Howards, sheltered therein.

Unfortunately contact had not been made to the left with the 9th Division, and after dark the enemy discovered the gap of almost 400 yards. Unopposed, they entered the quarry from the north and the rear and captured the brigade commander with two of the battalion COs, and quickly overran the whole excavation. Next day a counterattack to recapture the quarry failed, and the redoubtable divisional commander, General Capper, while up in the front line of the advance, was killed at the same time as the leading platoon commander of the 2nd Worcesters.

On the 7th's right the 1st Division advanced. The left brigade made good progress, the 10th Gloucesters and 8th Royal Berks penetrating half-a-mile inside the enemy lines, where the 1st Black Watch and 1st Camerons passed through them. These two battalions then reached the main road, Lens to La Bassée, a few men actually penetrating into Hulluch. But the right brigade failed badly, only just reaching the enemy's front-line trench. There enemy shelling greatly shook the men, and many of them, individually and in small groups, without orders, crawled back to their original trenches.

Next on the right was the well-known 15th (Scottish) Division. Its success was spectacular. The 7th KOSB went right round the northern side of Loos itself, and by 7.30 was over a mile inside the German lines. Its sister battalion, the 8th KOSB, did even better. It was called forward soon after zero hour and followed close behind the forward battalions. By 9.15 am it had passed through the 7th and was almost a mile to the east of Loos, having covered approximately 4 miles since leaving its starting line. By 8 am the whole of Loos was in British hands, fighting in the streets having been chaotic.

The MO of the 9th Black Watch, Captain Bearn, had a unique experience in Loos. He set up his regimental aid post in the cellar of a ruined house, in which a French woman and her daughter, aged seventeen, were living. These two women helped the doctor all day in binding up wounds and making tea. During the afternoon Captain Bearn discovered that a German sniper from a house nearby was firing at the party. The young French girl, Mademoiselle Moreau, seized the MOs revolver and disappeared. A few seconds later two shots were heard, and the sniping stopped. Mademoiselle Moreau returned to the cellar with the words 'C'est fini'. Later in the day, when the stream of wounded had decreased, the girl took Captain Bearn across the road and up the stairs of the house opposite and showed him the bodies of the two dead Germans she had shot.

Some days later the GOC heard of the incident and ordered Captain Bearn to go back into Loos, find the girl and bring her to Divisional Headquarters, where she was introduced to the general. Very soon she received the British Military Medal. Later she was awarded the Croix de Guerre and the medals of the British Red Cross, and the St John Ambulance Society. Maybe today in 1975 she is alive, at seventy-seven a reasonable probability.

The next division to the right, the 47th London Territorials were also successful. On the extreme right a row of dummy figures, laid in No Man's Land, were pulled erect by strings from the front-line trench after zero hour. They were taken by the enemy to be infantry advancing in the smoke and gas, causing them much useless expenditure of ammunition.

The leading battalions, the 7th London Regiment from Finsbury Square and the 6th from Farringdon Road, easily reached the Double Crassier held by the Germans 300 yards from their front-line trench with few casualties. Moving forward to the enemy's second line, they met stiff opposition. The 8th Londons and the Post Office Rifles went forward to support them, and the Rifles actually succeeded in climbing the Double Crassier.

The left brigade attacked with one battalion, the London Irish, kicking a football in front of them. They reached the enemy front line, and then by arrangement lay down while through them passed the 20th London (Blackheath and Woolwich) and the 19th (St Pancras).

The 20th had a great success, penetrating a mile inside the German lines and reaching a small copse and chalk pit well beyond the Double Crassier. Here A Company, under Captain Williams, captured two enemy field guns, which a few weeks later were on display on the Horse Guards Parade in London.

On the left the St Pancras battalion had a hard fight and were for a time held up across a cemetery, where they dug a makeshift trench. One of the battalion officers, Lt Pusch, was awarded the DSO for his work with the battalion's bombers, one of the only eight subalterns to win the DSO in World War I. Tragically he was killed in 1917. When darkness fell, the whole British battle line had been brought to a standstill.

During the latter half of 25 September the two reserve divisions, the 21st and 24th, were brought forward. These two divisions had never been in action, nor had they ever been in a trench. They were as well-trained infantrymen as less than a year's service would permit. They were not only inexperienced in battle but also in hardship, hunger and fatigue. They had spent the three previous nights in marching, through inefficient staff work, and the marching had been made more arduous by the lack of control of the transport, causing long delays. The brigade cookers had been left behind and the troops arrived on the battlefield in the afternoon of the 25th tired out, hungry and, now that the rain had started, wet. They had one consolation, however: they could see that much ground had been gained, and, even better, hundreds of prisoners marching back to captivity.

Progress was wearisome, the mud and obstacles unseen in the darkness impeded them and the ignorance of all ranks below brigade commanders of their mission sapped their confidence.

About 10 pm these two divisions passed over the original German front line and by 1 am had nearly reached the Loos–Haines road.

On the left the 24th got forward very well, and, crossing the Lens–La Bassée road, passed beyond it for three-quarters of a mile, the 8th Queens, 8th Buffs, 9th East Surreys and 8th West Kents reaching the German second line. The morale of these units had suddenly risen greatly, the men feeling that they were at least getting to grips with the enemy, the object for which they had rushed to join Kitchener's Army thirteen months before. Their hunger and discomforts of the preceding days were all forgotten. But the almost intact wire of the new German position halted them, and the four battalions, now in line, lay down in their farthest positions.

On the right the 21st Division also advanced at first, but then units from the forward brigade were seen withdrawing, for reasons unknown. The 9th and 10th KOYLI were sent to stiffen them, but coming under increasing fire, the whole division withdrew nearly back to the original British front line.

Seeing the retreat of the 21st Division, the 24th Division also started to withdraw. Something approaching panic now spread through these two very inexperienced divisions, and the situation map for the Battle of Loos at 4 pm on the 26th shows both of them streaming back from the front. It also shows the newly formed Guards Division arriving on the battlefield.

The Guards Division, formed in August 1915, consisted of the eight Guards battalions already serving on the Western Front, and a new battalion raised for each of the Grenadiers, Coldstream and Irish, together with an entirely new regiment – the Welsh Guards. The Division preserved the Guard's reputation for discipline, turn-out, and performance, and conditions of life in the trenches were to do little to harm its reputation.

On arrival at the battlefield it found that the 21st and 24th Divisions had left a gap of almost a mile, which it filled just after dark, about 9 pm. The next afternoon the Division attacked, and, after heavy fighting and casualties, reached the main road at Chalk Pit Wood, captured the previous day by the 9th East Surreys in their original penetration. Here the Guards established a line, and despite enemy counterattack, held it permanently. One of the two forward companies of the Irish Guards, who were holding Chalk Pit Wood, was commanded by Captain H. R. L.G. Alexander, later to be Field-Marshal Earl Alexander of Tunis. An eyewitness said that no one who saw the advance of the Guards at Loos will ever forget it. They moved forward slowly, relentlessly and in perfect order, and the sight of them did more than restore the confidence that had been shaken in the past thirty-six hours.

During the 27th and 28th counterattacks forced the three right-hand divisions back, and the shattered 15th Division was withdrawn from the line. Although its morale was still high, it had lost so many men, and its survivors were so tired, that it was considered unsafe to leave it where it might be counterattacked. The Division lost 216 officers killed, wounded or missing, and 6,400 men.

The ground today is very little altered from 1915, except that Fosse 8 and the mining buildings beside it have disappeared. Loos itself has been rebuilt on the old foundations of 1915, but there has been very little expansion.

The best way to see the Loos battlefield is to drive up the Lens–La Bassée road, N347. Just beyond the turning on the right to the little local aerodrome is an enormous cement factory on the left of the road. The building on the right of the main entrance stands where a small peasant's cottage stood in 1915, and from which the wood and its chalk pit run south-west. The cliff makes an excellent defensive position, and troops under the shelter of the steep bank would have been entirely protected from enemy shellfire from the east and south-east. The visitor must not be impressed by the size of the factory buildings, the area of chalk workings or the great heaps of spoil. None were there in 1915, and the little chalk pit is far more interesting.

Drive a mile further north along the main road and then turn left at a big crossroads from which roads branch off to Hulloch and Vermelles. Along the Vermelles road 600 yards a minor road leads off to the right for 300 yards. Just beyond where it peters out, and on the right, is the quarry where the brigade headquarters of the 7th Division was captured. Two battalions, perhaps more, could be sheltered in it. Again the visitor must take no notice of the gigantic coal tip towering above him. It did not exist in 1915.

Back on the main Lens–La Bassée road, drive into La Bassée over its canal. First left in the town and then, a mile on, left again brings one to the bridge over the canal. The towpath on the south bank opposite, along which Captain Kilby led his men, has been abandoned, but its track, now covered with long coarse grass and weeds, can be followed.

Loos is a nice clean little town. The Double Crassier is no longer in use, and its sides are being slowly covered with grass and undergrowth. The Tower Bridge is obviously comparatively new, its ancestor doubtless being so shaken by shellfire as to become rickety and unsafe. The new tower appears very similar in design to the 1915 edifice.

The cemetery where the St Pancras battalion was held up and had to dig themselves an elementary trench is easily found. Like all French cemeteries, the graves are covered with large and imposing marble headstones, or occasionally by large metal crosses. The troops must have disliked digging themselves in very much. The older part of the cemetery, that nearer Loos, contains many pre-1915 headstones, and today it seems that as good cover could have been obtained behind these large marble slabs as by entrenching.

The cost of Loos was high. Its credits were experience and, after a while, renewed morale.

16 Verdun: 1916

SITE *One of the great fortresses built to guard France's eastern frontier, vulnerable from across the Rhine, which flows north and south some 80 miles to the eastward. The town lies on the Route Nationale N3, Paris to Metz and on to Frankfurt, and is about 170 miles from Paris. The line of forts lies north-east, north, east and south-east of the town, and is about 6 miles out.*
CONTESTANTS *The French and German armies. No other nations took part, although the French had a coloured North African division.*
NUMBERS AND CASUALTIES *Impossible to estimate the numbers on each side but probably 3,000,000 men at one time or another took part. There were 700,000 casualties, almost equally divided between the two nations. A large proportion were killed.*

PRESENT ACCOMMODATION *There are good hotels in Verdun, the Bellevue in particular. Taxis are easily obtainable and the drivers, like those at Ypres, know the area well and can act as guides. A full day's touring is needed if a reasonable examination is to be made.*

In World War I Verdun carried the same prestige for France as Ypres did for the British Empire. The surrender of either would have been a blow to national morale.

Around Ypres the ground is flat and featureless, and its eastern perimeter, apart from a few villages and woods, possesses no natural defensive points. The defences of Verdun, however, were built on pronounced physical features, the ground to the east of the town being admirable for defence. Rising steeply from the river it forms broad uplands, the 'Heights of the Meuse', often 300 feet above the river, and then falls away very gradually eastward. On this eastern slope lay the circle of forts 6 miles out from the town and forming a 12-mile semicircle.

Each fort supported its neighbour; intervening valleys and depressions were tactically wired, fields of fire for both small arms and artillery were cleared. Trenches for the outposts were dug in front of the forts. Each fort, designed to resist a siege, was self-contained, and although the heavier guns had been removed before 1914, the forts remained immensely strong. Usually several hundred yards in circumference, they were rabbit warrens of gun emplacements, loopholes, food, water and ammunition stores, sleeping accommodation, command and observation posts, repair shops and so on. The overhead cover of brick, steel and concrete covered with earth and then turfed was strong enough to resist direct hits by any shell less than a 10-inch.

The fortress of Verdun, designed and built in peace-time for the defence of France, was one of the most important links in the inner circle of her eastern defences. Undoubtedly Verdun's long and successful resistance to the great enemy attacks in 1916 greatly influenced France's defensive strategy after 1919, focusing her military thinking on the old lines of forts, steel, concrete and wire. This living in the past found its fulfilment in the Maginot Line of 1940.

Ypres was always an active sector, but Verdun only came into the military limelight in 1916, when the Germans tried to capture what they rightly considered to be one of the great defensive bastions of France.

On 21 February, after a rather meagre bombardment of nine days, the enemy attacked the north and north-eastern sectors of the salient with six divisions. At midday on 21 February the enemy bombardment was violently stepped up. The assault was not launched until 5 pm and was then not altogether successful, two German divisions actually falling back to their start line during the night. Nevertheless, the French front line was penetrated in several places and many prisoners taken. By the 24th the Germans had advanced to a depth of 3½ miles in places, the second position was captured, and some unsteadiness had appeared in a North African Native Unit. The great Fort Douaumont fell, and that night the

French army group comamnder evacuated the great open slope to the east, which had not been attacked. The situation was very grave.

Next day General Pétain took command of the army group and the battle. Calm and imperturbable, he early looked to his communications, ensuring that reserves of men, ammunition, vehicles and stores could be unceasingly pumped into the apparently closing circle. The railway was repaired, dumps established, and the main artery, the road from Bar le Duc, was widened. Along these routes came all the means wherewith Pétain would hold and defeat the enemy. Lorries brought 1,700 loads every twenty-four hours into the sector by this road, which became known as La Voie Sacrée. Today its kilometre posts are small stone memorials, capped with concrete models of the French steel helmet decorated with a palm leaf, erected in honour of the countless soldiers who marched up it into Verdun but did not return.

By the 28th the resistance of the reinforced French garrisons had stiffened, and the German attack was temporarily halted. A few days later, however, the French sector across the river on the left bank of the Meuse and north-west of Verdun was also attacked.

At first this right flank attack was not unsuccessful, though the French infantry, at its best, resisted as gallantly as the Germans did on the Somme. Attacks frequently gaining only a few hundred yards laterally as well as in depth were extremely costly, and the enemy paid as heavy a price as the British did four months later. The villages were pulverised, roads disappeared, but gradually this attack ground to a halt.

In mid-April another great German advance south of Douaumont failed badly, though causing casualties to the French infantry, and soon afterwards General Nivelle, later to become for a very brief period Commander-in-Chief of the French army, and General Mangin arrived to strengthen Pétain's hand as army and corps commanders respectively. These three generals became the soul of the defence of Verdun, the embodiment of the famous cry of defiance, 'Ils ne passeront pas'.

Early in June a German attack, the last at Verdun, succeeded in surrounding Fort Vaux, the most easterly post in the then contracting circle. Since March the fort and its immediate surroundings had received an average of 8,000 shells a day, and all

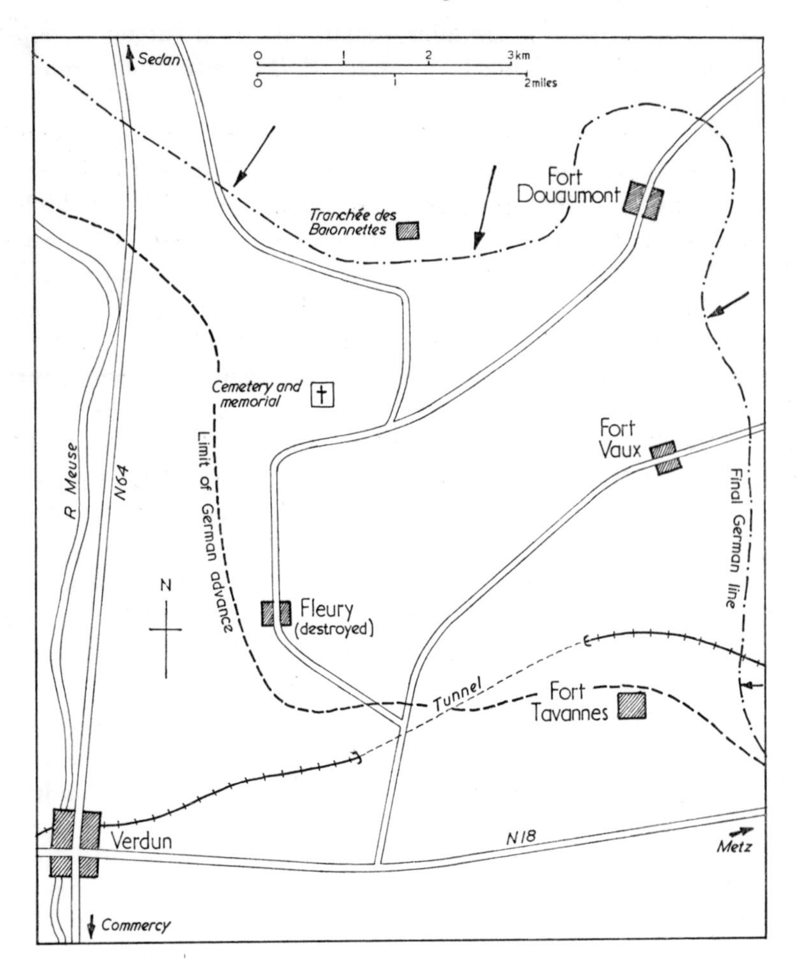

amenities of every sort, including sanitation, had gone. On 8 June Commandant Reynel and the garrison of 300 men surrendered. The French officer was received by the German Crown Prince, who congratulated him on the almost superhuman resistance of his men and his own brilliant leadership.

By the end of June the German 'Grand Assault' had petered out, largely because of the enormous loss of life. Its chief result was the limitation of the French contribution to the Allied attack on the Somme. The great offensive there, which began July 1916, brought relief to Verdun within ten days.

By October the French were able to counterattack, and on the

24th of that month General Mangin launched a four-division assault magnificently supported by the skilful handling of the bombardment. The two great forts of Douaumont and Vaux were recaptured, much of the ground lost in the previous months was regained and the venture became a moral victory as well as a tactical success. Seven weeks later Mangin attacked again on an even wider front and, penetrating 4 miles, practically re-established himself in the original front line. After ten months of fighting and appalling losses the Germans were back where they had started. The limelight was switched off and Verdun sank into obscurity until the end of the war.

The losses on both sides were gigantic. Germany lost from all causes 336,000 men while France had to sacrifice 362,000, almost half of whom were killed.

On approaching the north-east sector of the battlefield by the Avenue de la 42iemé Division, one sees that nature's repair work is evident everywhere. Clearly no attempt whatever has been made since 1918 to clear, cultivate or afforest the battlefield apart from the immediate vicinity of the villages, and a few yards' walk off the road into the woods takes the visitor on to the battlefield. The trees growing thereabouts, which clearly have not been planted by man, almost hide the signs of warfare. However, within a yard or two of the road one quickly stumbles over a shellhole or a shattered but still recognisable trench. Fifty years and more have covered the ground with a soft two-inch carpet of leaf mould, fir cones and pine needles, but the pronounced unevenness everywhere is unmistakable. In September 1961, within 15 yards of the road, a visitor picked up a French soldier's wine bottle, that indispensable piece of equipment that was refilled with 'vin rouge' nightly when the rations came up.

Soon after entering the forest on the road out to Fort Douaumont, one sees a large memorial to André Maginot. A sergeant in the French army, he was wounded at Verdun in November 1914. After the war he was elected to the National Assembly as 'Deputé de la Meuse'. Becoming Minister of War by 1920, he was responsible for the whole conception of the defence line that bore his name, and which so tragically misled the French people into thinking that they were safe in 1940.

In the centre of the battlefield, near the village of that name, lies Fort Douaumont. The fort is by no means a vast heap of rubble that might be expected from the terrific punishment it received. The outline is quite clear. Within, passages can be traversed and rooms visited, and the top, though much cut up by shellfire, still bears a semblance of flatness. A concrete observation post still protrudes from it. The domes of steel over the big guns that were removed in 1914 are still there, now worn smooth by countless visitors over the years. Numerous footpaths now exist between shellholes or the remains of projecting installations, and scraps of steel from exploded shells can still be picked up beside them. No cartridge cases are to be found, for all defensive small-arms fire came from machine-gun emplacements built into the walls. There was very little hand-to-hand fighting on or around the fort. For the French it was just a question of being shelled and shelled and shelled, and sticking it: for the Germans it was attack after attack upon the open slopes, with weighty artillery support and enormous casualties. Before 1916 the forts were protected by moats, which guarded the sheer walls of concrete, and although the moats and their outer escarpments were badly damaged by shellfire, the debris thrown against the main outer walls of Fort Douaumont helped to protect and strengthen them. They are still in remarkably good condition.

Inside the fort a guide conducts parties around those rooms and passages that can still be visited. Built in 1880, the workmanship of the fort is superb, and the inner stone walls, roofs, and floors today show little sign of warfare. One of the bigger rooms is now a museum, which includes an unexploded German 13-inch shell. The two old 'poilus' who act as guides and caretakers both fought here in 1916; they are intensely proud of their charge and their medals.

The ground around the fort and up to 300 yards out shows countless shellholes, so many of which are of large calibre. The thin covering of turf quite fails to hide these great indentations.

Standing on the roof of the fort and looking outward and downward to the north and north-east, one understands the problem of the attacking German infantry. An advance of 800 yards over completely open ground and up a considerable slope already cut up by shellfire seems in the face of heavy defensive machine-gun fire and shrapnel to be almost an impossible task.

The German supporting fire, intended to keep the defenders' heads down, would not be so effective as against open trenches, and the iron and steel cover over the defending machine-gun emplacements must have afforded the French infantry great moral support as well as material protection.

Fort Vaux, though considerably smaller than Fort Douaumont, is very similar to it. The inward facing wall of the courtyard carries a plaque commemorating the last pigeon flown out by Commandant Reynel, which bore a message asking for help, water and rations, and stated that the Commandant could get no reply from the neighbouring forts.

On looking over the battlefield from these two forts, one is impressed by the skill of the French generals who first sited them. They created such widespread fields of fire on the forward aprons that the attacker was forced into the open and the defender given perfect observation. The second and greater impression is of the bravery which the junior officers and their men, both French and German, must have shown in their respective tasks during these operations, the French defenders enduring almost unendurable persecution by ceaseless shellfire, the Germans advancing uphill against fearful odds.

North of Verdun lies the great cemetery, where 15,000 men, mostly French, are buried. It occupies a gently rising slope, at the top of which stands the vast and imposing memorial building to the 130,000 missing. It can be seen for miles. From a central hall radiate two large wide cloisters, whose walls have alcoves carrying the names of the missing men. Over the central hall rises an enormous tower, from whose summit a light burns throughout the night. Lit at dusk, it revolves slowly, illuminating every sector in turn.

Perhaps the most tragic and certainly the most romantic spot on the whole of the 1914–18 Western Front is the Tranchée des Baionnettes. Early in June 1916 a French platoon of one officer and about twenty men were preparing to meet from their front-line trench just out in front of Douaumont what was the last successful German attack in the Battle of Verdun. Their bayonets fixed, they sheltered against the parapet of their trench, being heavily shelled. A German 13-inch gun dropped a shell 15 yards in front of the trench, its explosion killing all the platoon by shock.

The tons of loose earth and debris thrown up fell on the trench, completely filling it and burying the crouching soldiers and their rifles. The fixed bayonets, however, stuck up above the fallen earth and can be seen there today. The attacking Germans passed by the trench and left it undisturbed, while the French counter-attack of October also left it undamaged. By the generosity of an American, George Raud, a strong concrete arcade was built over the trench in 1919 to preserve it. However, souvenir hunters started their depredations and now a strong wire fence keeps visitors a few feet back. Projecting from the 30-yard long mound can be seen several bayonets sticking out of the earth and the muzzles of a few rifles from which the bayonets have been stolen. Also on the grave may be seen a few cheap trinkets and coins thrown by visitors and pilgrims. The trinkets and coins are periodically collected and sold for the French Red Cross. Few visitors seem to talk as they walk back to their cars.

17 Vimy Ridge: 1917

SITE *North-west of Arras on the Arras–Lens Road, N25, and west of the small town of Vimy.*
CONTESTANTS *The Canadian Corps of four divisions under General Byng with 15,000 men. Part of 6th German Army (ten battalions totalling 5,000 men), reinforced by five other battalions.*
CASUALTIES *The Canadians lost 1,600 killed and 5,500 wounded. German losses are unknown.*

PRESENT ACCOMMODATION *The Hotel de L'Univers in Arras is excellent. Although it is in the centre of town, it is entirely secluded from noise, and the reception staff are well accustomed to arranging day tours and chartering taxis to take visitors to the Ridge.*

The town of Arras has always been tactically important. The River Scarpe flows through it on its eastward course to join the Scheldt, and immediately to its north-west is Vimy Ridge. Until this century the river had few bridges above or below the town, and the single crossing there, together with the ridge, directed all east and west movements, whether commercial, historical or military, through the town.

The Ridge, almost 400 feet above the plain of Douai to the east, extends for 3 miles in a roughly south-east to north-west direction. On its south-west face the slope is an easy gradient rarely calling for a change of gear, but the north-east face is very steep. Indeed, for one stretch of almost 2 miles, the escarpment is so severe that no road is possible and the pedestrian, on his downward climb, has to tread carefully to avoid a sprained ankle.

The Ridge has figured as a tactical feature influencing military moves for centuries. The Romans on their way to Boulogne to invade Britain in 55 BC passed through Cambrai, Arras and St Pol, and the great motor road today, the N39 follows the exact trace of their road.

The French, although losing the Battle of Malplaquet in 1709, had inflicted enormous casualties on Marlborough's Allied army. Louis XIV and his general, Villars, decided on a planned withdrawal towards Paris, refusing battle and forcing Marlborough to pursue them. Villars took up a series of defensive and delaying positions, one of which, extending north and south of Arras, had its left wing along Vimy Ridge overlooking the great plain of Douai. Marlborough, seeing a great French army formed up on the Ridge and immediately in front of it the steep escarpment, changed direction and veered off to the south, sensibly avoiding action on such unfavourable terrain.

Vimy Ridge is best known, however, for its prominence in World War I. From October 1914 the Germans occupied the Ridge for two and a half years, until they were driven off it by the Canadians in April 1917.

The Ridge figured in yet another tactical operation in 1940 during the British withdrawal to Dunkirk. An unsuccessful counter-attack southward by the 5th and 50th British Divisions, then holding the Ridge, was launched to cut the lines of communication of the German armoured thrust to Abbeville, Boulogne and Calais, unsuccessfully.

In 1917 the German front-line trenches on Vimy Ridge were usually a few hundred yards down the south-west face, so that they often had less than 500 yards of defensive depth, and then the near precipice, behind them. They dug caves in this eastward-facing wall for shelters, cookhouses, headquarters, etc. Owing to the steepness of the escarpment, no Allied gunfire could touch them, and they lived in great comfort and safety. Half a mile back from the Ridge they dug a second, very strong, line.

In April 1917 the Canadian Corps of four divisions attacked the enemy lines on Vimy Ridge. Before the great attack the Canadians had built a great network of tunnels in the easily worked chalk of the Ridge. Those leading back from close behind the front line, were for shelter, cooking, storehouses and communications back to battalion or brigade headquarters. Some are still there, a quarter of a mile long, and the whole almost make up an underground town. But those dug forward were for a very different purpose. They penetrated under the enemy's lines, and when the great attack started, their heads, crammed with explosives, were blown up, allowing Canadian soldiers to emerge and engage the German second line. In some areas the opposing front-line trenches were only 100 yards apart.

The advance, despite heavy snow, went well, and the explosions of the mines, together with the tremendous artillery barrage did much to overawe the defending Germans. On the extreme left

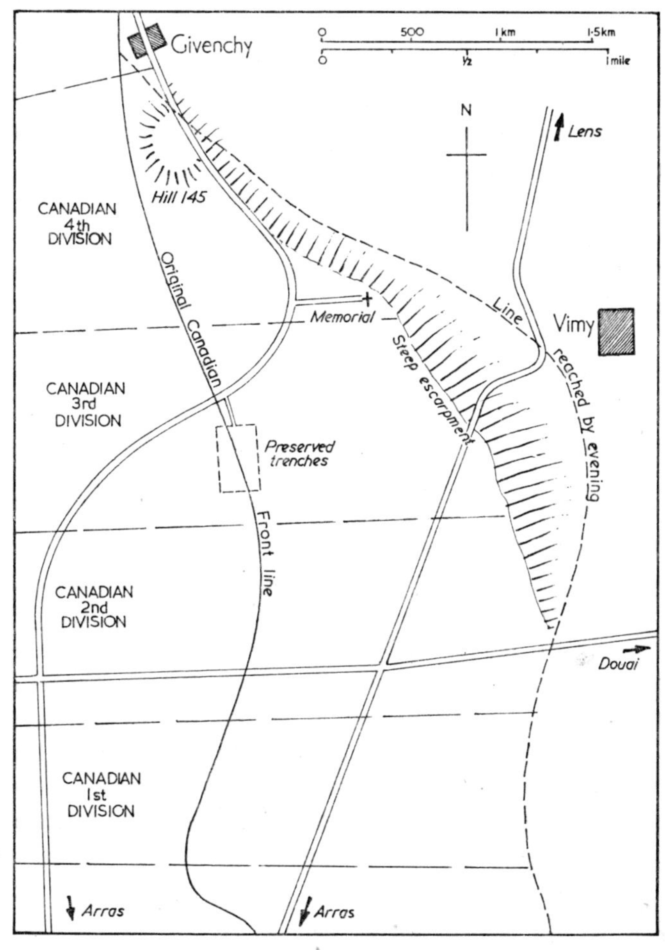

Hill 145, the highest point of the Ridge, gave much trouble, and the 4th Canadian Division swarming around it failed to reach its summit. In the centre the 2nd and 3rd Canadian Divisions had a very easy passage; by midday they had reached the crest of the Ridge and were looking over the plain, watching the fleeing Germans. On the right the 1st Canadian Division had an equally great victory. Canadian casualties were so light in comparison with similar affairs elsewhere that it was apparent the defenders were defeated by the artillery preparation and the mines before the Canadians left their trenches. Rarely can it be said that a battle goes according to plan, but the attack of the 1st, 2nd and 3rd Divisions at Vimy is the exception that proves the rule.

For a few hours, and before the Germans could react to the reverse in their usual swift fashion, there was an open breach in the line that a large force of cavalry could have exploited. Instead, only two patrols, each of one officer and ten men, went out on reconnaissance, achieving little.

Seeing the successful Canadians capturing the remainder of the Ridge, the Germans holding the 4th Division on Hill 145 retreated, and that night the four divisions moved down the slope on to the plain and there dug a new line. Four days later they advanced to the main enemy second line about 3 miles from the crest. The 3rd Division finished nearly 5 miles beyond its original front-line trench.

Two hours are ample to visit the battlefield of Vimy Ridge. They will be well spent.

On the road up to the Canadian Monument there is a signpost indicating a brief diversion, which is well worth taking. A very short walk from the little car park brings one to a short stretch of the Canadian front-line trenches. They have been most imaginatively preserved by what appears to be the original sandbagging. The original trench walls, or what remained of them in 1919, were refaced with ordinary sandbags filled with concrete. The canvas has long since rotted away, and the concrete, still bearing the imprint of the canvas weave, gives a convincing impression of originality. To informed old soldiers, however, they are obvious but very moving substitutes for the originals. Their only drawbacks are their symmetry, perfect alignment and cohesion. No trenches had any of these qualities.

All round these preserved trenches is an area several hundred yards square covered in well-kept turf and containing hundreds of large and small hollows – the shellholes. Walking among them needs care: rarely can one find five or six paces of level going, and constant attention, with eyes down, is essential to avoid stumbling and falling. Many fir trees grow in this area, but the visitor desirous of recapturing the atmosphere of the trenches must remember that there were none in 1917.

A quarter of a mile further on at the top of the Ridge stands the great memorial to the Canadians who lost their lives at Vimy. Twenty acres of turf have been laid round the monument and every sign of war has been obliteratd. Shellholes and trenches have been smoothed over and all war debris removed. The turf nearer to the monument is cut by mowing, while the outer stretches are similar to the 'cut-rough' of a well-kept golf course. The view over the plain of Douai to the east is magnificent, but it should be noted that most of the many vast slagheaps from the coalmines in the distance were not there in 1917.

Index